Teaching Writing Genres Across the Curriculum

Strategies for Middle School Teachers

A volume in
Contemporary Language Education
Series Editor: Terry A. Osborn, University of Connecticut

Contemporary Language Education

Terry A. Osborn, *University of Connecticut*
Series Editor

Teaching Writing Genres Across the Curriculum

Strategies for Middle School Teachers

Edited by

Susan Lee Pasquarelli
Roger Williams University

INFORMATION AGE
PUBLISHING

Greenwich, Connecticut 06830 • www.infoagepub.com

Library of Congress Cataloging-in-Publication Data

Teaching writing genres across the curriculum : strategies for middle school teachers / edited by Susan Lee Pasquarelli.
   p. cm. – (Contemporary language education)
 Includes bibliographical references and index.
 ISBN 1-59311-421-4 (pbk.) – ISBN 1-59311-422-2 (hardcover)
 1. English language–Composition and exercises–Study and teaching (Middle school) I. Pasquarelli, Susan Lee. II. Contemporary language education (Greenwich, Conn.)
 LB1631.T343 2006
 808.042'0712–dc22

                                         2005033439

Printed in the United States of America

*This book is dedicated to the middle school students
who participated in our investigations of teaching genre by genre.
They were our real teachers.*

ACKNOWLEDGMENTS

Many colleagues contributed to the production of this book. First I thank Tim Reagan, former dean of the School of Education, at Roger Williams University, who so loved the idea of a graduate student book project, he personally helped pursue a publisher for this volume and was our head cheerleader throughout the writing process. I also thank Rachel McCormack, for providing her scholarly expertise and support during the writing; Linda Gambrell, for the wise knowledge she provided to the Master of Arts in Literacy program development as well as her kind words in the foreword of this book; Terry Osborn, our series editor, who taught us the tricks of the trade; and all the Master of Arts in Literacy graduate students who participated in the genre study summer workshops that helped inform the chapters in this book.

I give special thanks to Nantucket teachers, Karla Butler and Anne Perkins, and Newport teacher, Kate Canole, for generously offering their middle school classes to try out some of our genre material; and, the Roger Williams University Research Foundation for funding two writing research projects that helped us make sense of the culture of the writing classroom.

Finally, all of the authors and the editor wish to thank our families and friends for patience and support as we juggled the demands of teaching and the writing of this book.

CONTENTS

CONTENTS

FOREWORD

This book could not have been conceived at a better time. Its content takes on special meaning at a time when middle grades literacy instruction is receiving national attention. The underlying theme of this book is that teaching students the form and function of genre is a way to help all students become more proficient writers. What is unique about this book is that the teaching of each genre is embedded in the writing process.

Learning to write well is arguably a complex task. Becoming a proficient writer requires experiences that help make the meaning and importance of written communication transparent. This book takes an important step toward closing the gap between the research on writing and productive classroom practice in the middle grades. Good writing instruction requires active involvement and engagement to ensure that the joy, pleasure, and value of writing are appreciated. The teachers who contributed to this volume provide in-depth treatment of each genre and address the issues facing middle grades teachers about how to teach writing in a motivating and meaningful way. The voices of these teachers and their students add interest, depth, and credibility to this excellent text. Most important, this book is grounded in theory and research, yet it maintains a clear focus on the day-to-day instructional practices in schools.

This volume examines genres and the strategies that teachers can use to develop writing proficiency in all students. The chapters guide teachers, step by step, in providing effective, engaging writing instruction, genre by genre. Exemplary teaching strategies are clearly depicted and illustrated with wonderful samples of student work. Each chapter focuses on a particular genre along with model instructional practices, and steps needed to ensure that the instructional practices can be effectively adopted in the

Teaching Writing Genres Across the Curriculum, pages xi–xii
Copyright © 2006 by Information Age Publishing
All rights of reproduction in any form reserved.

middle grade classroom. In addition, each chapter highlights sample lessons, showing how writing can be prompted, modeled, or demonstrated by the teacher. These specific genre lessons enable us to think more deeply about writing instruction and the writing process.

The reality is that our schools should be providing middle grades students with instruction that will improve the quality of their writing. Our students have the right to instruction that builds both the skill and will to write increasingly complex narrative and expository material. This book ensures that writing instruction will become an integral part of the literacy agenda for middle grades teachers and students. It is an indispensable resource for teachers, teacher educators, school leaders, administrators, policymakers, and other educators who place a high priority on the literacy development and writing proficiency of our students.

The public awareness of the need for our students to be highly literate has never been greater. Fortunately, the knowledge base for improving writing instruction has never been richer. This book will serve as a valuable, practice-oriented text for in-service teachers and those in graduate-level writing courses. It will enhance the knowledge and skills of teachers who are committed to helping middle grades students become more literate.

—Linda B. Gambrell, Professor
Clemson University
Eugene T. Moore School of Education

CHAPTER 1

THE PRACTICE OF TEACHING GENRE BY GENRE

Susan Lee Pasquarelli

INTRODUCTION

For many years I have been working as a literacy specialist with middle school teachers' explorations of writing across the curriculum. Through these content area teachers' candid and direct accounts, I often hear that they are expected to provide writing instruction, although they have little or no preparation for teaching different types of expository and narrative writing. Their appeal for help eventually led to my experimenting with various methods for teaching writing genre by genre across the middle school curriculum.

Since I am a university professor, it was natural to bring my lessons learned in the middle schools to my university literacy courses. Last summer, I presented genre teaching to my graduate students enrolled in a Master of Arts in Literacy Program. Step by step, I took them through the process of teaching a genre to prepare middle school students for topic, purpose, and audience selection; organization of ideas; lead and thesis writing; how to improve author's voice; and, the writing process in general. As a course assignment, I asked my students to develop their own set of instructional materials and methods for teaching one specific genre. This book is the result of that assignment.

Teaching Writing Genres Across the Curriculum, pages 1–14
Copyright © 2006 by Information Age Publishing
All rights of reproduction in any form reserved.

Included in the chapters of this book is the work of eight hard-working middle school teachers who are convinced that teaching students the form and function of genre is a way to help all students meet state and national standards.

In this chapter, you will be introduced to the rationale and overall process for teaching genre by genre, one important lesson to introduce any genre, and a simple guide to using the chapters in this book.

RATIONALE FOR TEACHING A GENRE STUDY

I often explain to my graduate students that current writing practice suggests three components to teaching a writing program (Calkins, 1994; Graves, 1983; Weaver, 1996). They include the following: (a) the recursive stages of the writing process—planning, drafting, revising, editing, publishing, and sharing; (b) the English language arts conventions (grammar, spelling, and mechanics); and (c) the nature of each writing genre. To many teachers, administering the writing program is a daunting task. Through my experimentation in the schools, I have discovered that by teaching one writing genre at a time, it is possible to collapse all three components into one cohesive instructional process. Why not teach students to plan, draft, revise, and edit as they learn one specific genre? Why not teach grammar in the context of editing or literary elements in the context of the revision process? As a result, the entire writing program can be delivered through the identification and implementation of one genre. Figure 1.1 illustrates this concept by breaking down the traditional writing process stages to include all components of a particular writing genre.

As you peruse Figure 1.1, you will notice that guiding students through a genre study takes time, multiple teaching steps, and patience. There are, however, benefits to this approach. I have found that teaching a writing genre in this explicit, direct way improves students' dispositions toward writing, clarifies the different elements of genre, and improves writing achievement in general.

Because we have embedded the teaching of each genre into the "writing process," it is important to present our understanding of the nature of the writing process.

THE RECURSIVE NATURE OF THE WRITING PROCESS

As you consider teaching a genre study, it is important to note that although you will sequence your lessons from the planning stage to the publishing stage, the process a writer uses is by no means linear in nature.

Sequence of Teaching a Writing Genre

1. Have students **read an exemplary piece** written in the genre you are teaching to help their understanding of what the genre "looks like."

2. Using the inquiry method of instruction, have students **debrief the elements** or characteristics of the genre by going back to the model essay and combing the piece for various elements.

3. Teach the students to **PLAN** the genre:
   - Model **topic selection** and have students engage in guided and independent practice.
   - Model **purpose definition** and have students engage in guided and independent practice.
   - Model **audience selection** and have students engage in guided and independent practice.
   - Model **writing leads** and have students engage in guided and independent practice.
   - Model **verbal rehearsal** and have students engage in guided practice with one peer.
   - Model **brainstorming and recording ideas** for the essay into a graphic organizer and have students engage in guided and independent practice.
   - Remind students that planning takes place at any stage of the writing process.

4. Teach students to **DRAFT** the writing piece.
   - Model **drafting** the essay and have students engage in guided and independent practice.
   - Remind students that drafting takes place at any stage of the writing process.

5. Teach students to **REVISE** the writing piece.
   - Model how to **self-revise** for ideas and have students engage in peer and teacher conferencing.
   - Teach **revision mini-lessons** as needed.
   - Have students work on **multiple drafts** using revision strategies.
   - Remind students that revision takes place at any stage of the writing process.

6. Teach students to **EDIT** the writing piece.
   - Model how to **proofread** for grammar/mechanics and have students engage in peer-teacher conference for final editing.
   - Teach **editing mini-lessons** as needed.
   - Remind students that editing takes place at any stage of the writing process.

7. Teach students to **PUBLISH** their pieces.
   - Students **make final changes** and then prepare title pages, graphs, charts, etc.

8. Provide students with opportunities to **SHARE** their writing.
   - Students make their writing public through sharing aloud in class or exhibiting piece in library or classroom.

9. **EVALUATE** the writing piece.
   - Ask students to **self-evaluate** their pieces with a rubric scoring scale.
   - **Evaluate** your students' pieces with a rubric scoring scale.
   - Have the writer **set goals** based on the evaluation.

Figure 1.1.   Sequence of teaching a writing genre.

Researchers on writing have suggested that writers, in an authentic context, use a recursive process to produce a writing piece (Hayes, 2000; Hayes & Flower, 1980). For example, as I am writing this chapter, I sometimes discontinue drafting and return to what I wrote earlier to revise and edit that section. Once, however, that I have completed my draft, I will go back to revise for word choice, sentence and paragraph structure, and add and/or delete as I see fit. I call this my "final revision." Again, once my final revision is complete, I will go back to the revised draft for a "final edit" or final proofreading step. Likewise, while I am teaching a genre study, beginning with planning and concluding with final publishing, I encourage my students to go back to any step at any time as they see fit. Once students feel that they have a worthwhile draft, once again, I encourage them to go back for a final revision and proofread.

Although all writing processes are important and each work toward advancing the writing piece, I have found that when middle school students are left on their own to produce a piece, they often skip the *planning* or prewriting step. I have also discovered that when teaching a specific genre, the planning step is vital to the development of the piece because it is in that step that the elements of the genre take shape. For example, think about how one must approach the task of writing a research paper as opposed to writing a historical fiction account. The first is expository writing and the second is narrative writing. The first requires brainstorming ideas about facts; the second requires brainstorming about characters and plot. Although the approach to each has some common elements, essentially the planning stage is very different based on the nature of the genre.

As you work your way through teaching some or all of the genres in this book, you will find that the planning steps match the intended genre. In order for your students to understand the planning steps presented in this volume, it is important that you teach them the principles upon which they were developed. Following is a teaching event I have used successfully for students to understand the importance of the thinking processes an author uses while planning the purpose of a writing piece. This teaching event is intended to be an introduction to the teaching of all genres and is not included in other chapters of this book.

TEACHING EVENT FOR PLANNING A WRITING PIECE

Determining the Purpose of the Piece

Kyle, a 6th grader, taught me a valuable lesson about writing and the teaching of writing. The importance of having students engage in purposeful writing was brought home by his adolescent responses to a punitive writing task assigned as a result of a disruptive middle school team meeting.

As the story goes, Kyle was in a 6th grade team meeting in which many of the students were occupied in distracting the rest of the group. In an attempt to have students apologize for the unmanageable meeting, the teachers asked each student to write a 250-word apology letter to the team's teachers. Kyle's first attempt to write his letter is included below verbatim.

> Dear Red One Teacher, Mr. B., the guidance office, and the library.
>
> I am very very very sorry about how I and my classmates/peers acted during the team meeting we had this afternoon around twelve-thirty. Mr. B. was having a team meeting he had had with several other teams during the course of this week and last. I am truely, very very, very sorry about the very, very, very rude interuptions that I and my classmates/peers made this afternoon during the team meeting that Mr. R was giving in the IMC room this affternoon around twelve-thirty. I am truely, truely, very very, very, very, very, very sorry about what happened this affternoon around twelve-thirty.

Apparently Kyle wrote as much as he could to fulfill the assignment with the required word count, and, in disgust, complained to his mom (a colleague of mine) that he was unable to complete the letter because he was not one of the disruptive students. She suggested that he should write his true feelings in the letter as opposed to the suggested content. Kyle considered his mom's advice and worked hard to produce his second attempt, which is presented below.

> Dear Mr. B., Mr. T., Mr. W. and Ms. R.,
>
> I did not finish the assignment because I feel I had no need to start it. I have done nothing wrong and feel that the punishment is ridiculous. The fact that some kids are recidivists does not give you the right to make all the kids suffer through underserved punishment. I also hope you realize that making kids write for punishment is teaching them to hate writing.

When I present Kyle's letters to graduate students, middle school teachers, and even middle school students, it only takes them a few moments to understand that the difference between Kyle's first and second attempts was related to "purpose." In the first, since Kyle did not feel that he participated in the disturbance, he had no *purpose* for writing. In the second attempt, his purpose was clearly to inform his teachers that he was not part of the problem at school that day. Notice how Kyle's writing changed significantly in deliberateness of expression, clarity, and word choice. One cannot help but be impressed with the change in Kyle's sophisticated vocabulary (recidivists!), as well as his final advice to all teachers: "I also hope you realize that making kids write for punishment is teaching them to hate writing."

When working with middle school teachers and students, I have discovered that the purpose-setting step is often ignored. To persuade teachers and students to think about purpose, I only have to use Kyle's letter to illustrate my point.

So how do we teach purpose? When asking students to state the purpose of the piece, I ask them to identify the purpose as an infinitive verb. Are they writing *to tell? To clarify? To persuade? To appeal? To encourage? To entertain? To make people laugh? To teach?*

Think back to Kyle's writing, his first attempt at letter writing was "to apologize."When he attempted to write a letter to fulfill that purpose, his writing was repetitive and uninteresting. However, when he had an authentic purpose for writing, "to inform," his piece took on a vivid new voice.

As you use this book to teach genre studies, you will notice that each author provides a purpose-setting step in the planning stage.

Determining an Audience

Identifying an audience for writing is another often forgotten instructional step. Determining an audience accomplishes two tasks. First it helps writers understand for whom they are writing, and secondly it helps writers identify the level of background knowledge and detail that must be included in the piece (Hayes, 2000). Although the concept of audience is complex, for middle school writers, I suggest they decide two things about audience *before* they begin composing:

1. Who will be reading this piece? If the students' answer to this question is "friends," then maybe they will use informal speech. If their readers were teachers, they would probably use more formal language.

2. What is the audience's level of knowledge? The second consideration with audience includes the prior knowledge the readers have of the topic. Students need to think about: Am I writing for readers with *little or no* background knowledge about my topic? Or Am I writing for readers with *much* background knowledge about my topic? Just recently, as I was explaining this concept to a group of 6th graders, one student excitedly jumped up and said:

   > "Oh! I get it. If I were writing my research paper on the extinction of ocelots for my friends, I wouldn't use any of the BIG terms, but if I were writing for someone with lots of knowledge of extinction, I could use the big words that they already know."

I have found that once students begin to investigate the concepts of purpose and audience, they cannot help but consider word choice or the level of detail they will use in their writing pieces.

Purpose + Audience = Word Choice

Writing researchers and practitioners have often asserted that writers need to consider the juxtaposition of purpose setting and audience selection. Johnson (2000) contends that when writers consider both together, the writer attends to appropriate vocabulary and or word choice. I often explain to my young writers that if they were going to write emails to their friends to inquire about the evening homework, they most likely would use slang and other informal words. Then I ask them to consider what type of word choice they would use if they were going to write the same email to their teachers. After such consideration, students often begin to grasp the relationship of purpose, audience, and word choice.

To enhance students' understanding of purpose, audience, and word choice, I suggest you begin your writing instruction by having students engage in a learning event that my colleague, Rachel McCormack, and I adapted (Hairston & Ruszkiewicz, 1991) and have used extensively in our grade 4 through 12 classroom work (McCormack & Pasquarelli, 1998). For this learning event, you will need the following items:

1. Brochures from a *wide* variety of sources, including (a) those that advertise entertainment (art museums, historical places and museums, other educational and noneducational places to visit, environmental science expeditions, whale watching, etc.), (b) those that inform (dangers of lead poisoning, prevention of Lyme disease, importance of exercise, etc), and (c) those that offer services (magazine subscriptions, exercise classes, library services, etc.). You will need three brochures per student in your class, each representing different purposes.

2. Enough handouts for all students and one transparency of Figure 1.2.

Type of Brochure	Purpose of Brochure	Intended Audience	Word Choice

Figure 1.2.   Brochure activity recording sheet.

The steps to implement the lesson follow:

1. Explain to students that you are going to have them engage in an inquiry activity designed to have them become better writers. Tell them that you are going to have them analyze brochures for the writing content, and, at the end of the activity, you will reveal a very important writing principle. Hand out three brochures to each student each representing a different purpose. For example, I make sure that each student receives an entertainment brochure, an information brochure, and a general service brochure.

2. Next model for students how to analyze the brochures. Your goal is to have students identify the type of brochure, its purpose (to inform, to persuade, to teach, etc.), its intended audience, and the key words the author uses to appeal to the audience. On a transparency made from Figure 1.2, model for students how to extract the purpose of the brochure, the audience intended, and the key words the author used to get his point across. Your modeling will look something like this:

Type of Brochure	Purpose of Brochure	Intended Audience	Word Choice
Whale-watching	To *persuade* families to go on a day long whale watch	Families, especially parents Teachers	• Educationally valuable! • Fun! • Discount rates • Pleasurable
Lyme Disease	To *inform* people of the dangers of Lyme disease and how to prevent getting it.	Parents Teachers Adults (general public)	• Dangerous • Preventative measures • Side effects • Scientific evidence • Statistics

3. Next ask students to analyze the three brochures while you walk around the room aiding their investigations.

4. After students have completed the recording sheet, ask a few students to share their responses. Fill out your transparency with their offerings being careful to ask for information from a variety of types of brochures. When your matrix is completed on the overhead, you may have five to six types of brochures with a variety of purposes listed.

5. Next point to the headings on the transparency: purpose, audience, and word choice. Ask students if they can interpret the purpose of

this activity by writing a word equation demonstrating the relationship among the ideas. Ultimately you are asking students to determine that *purpose + audience = word choice.*

6. Finally, explain to students that they will always be using this equation while considering writing their pieces.

We have had much success with using this learning event to bring home the concepts of identifying a clear purpose, selecting a distinct audience, and thinking of the type of word choice appropriate to each writing piece. As you teach each genre, you can remind students of this activity and the importance of considering purpose and audience. In each chapter of this book, you will find both a purpose and audience selection activity designed specifically for each genre.

The lesson I have presented above teaches young authors to be aware of many important writing principles: setting purposes, maintaining a consistent audience, and identifying important vocabulary. Following is the overview of the process of teaching a genre that you will find in this book.

HOW TO TEACH A GENRE STUDY

Planning

As you use this book to help you teach each genre, you will notice how each chapter encourages a long planning process. We have been diligent to identify and clarify multiple mini-lessons to help students think about planning their writing genre in a thoughtful way.

First, each author introduces the genre to students by providing them with a model essay to read. Often teachers ask students to participate in a new writing event without providing them with an exemplary piece to familiarize them to what the genre "looks like." As a result, students do not have a conceptualization of the genre.

Also included in every chapter of this volume is how to determine a clear purpose for the intended genre, choose a topic and audience, write a lead and thesis statement, and identify an organizing structure before composing begins. We have established that if we do a thorough job of teaching students to plan their specific genre pieces, the final products accomplish the following: (a) address a specific audience, (b) maintain a consistent purpose throughout, and (c) are organized and cohesive.

Drafting

In this volume, we encourage students to draft without concern or worry for conventions or perfect word choice (Calkins, 1994). We explain that the process of drafting is to put our broad ideas on paper and roughly compose the piece from the beginning to the end. We have found that some students prefer to write some of the draft and revise that piece before they continue drafting. As you recall, that is the nature of the recursive writing process. At any stage, the writer can revise and/or edit or go all the way back to the planning step if necessary. Once students have become familiar with the writing process, we allow their personal preferences to prevail.

Revising

Graves (1983) suggests that revising is the act of improving ideas, word choice, and the writing piece in general. Some of the chapters in this volume offer revision suggestions specific to the genre. As you recall, the act of revision can take place at any stage of the writing process. We also advocate that once a draft is complete, students, as a matter of course, self-revise, and confer with peers and teacher to aid their revision suggestions (Graves, 1983).

Editing

As you use this book, you will notice that each author suggests that you teach grammar in the context of editing (Weaver, 1996). Thus, grammar instruction is presented as "fix-up" editing strategies. We have had much success in improving the English language arts conventions through this method. As with revision, we once again advocate that first students self-edit and then confer with peers and teacher to aid the editing process (Graves, 1983).

Publishing and Sharing

One of the reasons behind the long established practice of having students publish and share their work is to ensure that students truly understand the concept of audience (Bereiter & Scadamalia, 1987). Calkins (1994) designed the "author's chair" as an opportunity to have young authors share their work within the context of a writers' community. By making the author's chair a regular practice, students will be more likely to *picture* the audience for whom they are writing *while* they are writing.

Evaluating

For each genre presented in this book, we have included an evaluation rubric in Appendix A. As students are working on their drafts of each genre, you can present the rubric to illustrate your expectations of their work in each category. It is essential that students understand the evaluation process *before* they finish the writing piece. As students peer revise and edit, they may wish to have a copy of the rubric handy to refer to throughout the process of multiple draft writing.

As a final evaluation tool, you may then apply the rubric giving students a score for each bullet within each category. We have been careful to provide you with analytic rubrics that will, in the end, help you and your students determine the *strengths* and *needs* of the writing piece. To tally the score within each category, average the scores students earned on each bullet and then average the category scores to come up with a final score. We have also included a score conversion chart in Appendix A if your school requires you to assign letter grades.

USING THIS BOOK TO TEACH GENRE BY GENRE

Throughout this volume, you will be presented with tried and true genre teaching events. The graduate students who contributed to this volume experimented with their own middle school classes to bring you an experienced point of view. In addition, I have also used these or similar teaching events in my interactions with middle school students.

In Chapter 2, Barlow and Francis present a comprehensive step-by-step approach to the teaching of the narrative account. They have set their model narrative account in an historical context, but explain a variety of content areas in which the narrative account would be useful to extend the curriculum. Toward the end of their chapter, they provide a very clear teaching event for a revision strategy of adding sensory details to the writing piece. This revision strategy will also be useful while revising the narrative procedure, the persuasive essay, the reflective essay, and the feature newspaper account. Additionally, they include an exemplary peer feedback form to aid students' peer conferences during the revision process. This form is adaptable for use in any genre.

In Chapter 3, Fernandes and Labrecque have combined their work on the teaching of the persuasive essay to help you troubleshoot the most difficult aspects of the genre. Their exemplary model essay is written in the context of an environmental science topic, but they provide information on why the persuasive essay is an authentic genre for use across the middle school curriculum. Of particular interest in their chapter is an extensive lesson on how to use a graphic organizer to help plan the persuasive rough draft.

In Chapter 4, Dunbar has presented her new approach to having her 6th graders write a feature newspaper article in the context of a social studies class. Her exceptional topic selection methods and outstanding model essay will give you an idea on how to use this genre in any given content area. She has also included an important teaching event to help you work with students on selecting an "angle" for their articles, an element that is very specific to the genre of feature article writing.

In Chapter 5, Canole presents an intricate plan for teaching the narrative procedure. Her model essay is aptly named, "How to Write a Narrative Procedure." In essence, she used her model essay to outline for students what is involved in writing a narrative procedure. Canole has included a detailed lesson plan on topic selection for the narrative account that takes students from a very broad topic to a narrow topic. Particularly of note in her chapter is an extension on the *purpose + audience = word choice* lesson that is specific to the genre she is presenting.

In Chapter 6, Scallin neatly outlines a clear teaching process for writing mathematical responses to open-ended questions. A math teacher for many years, Scallin learned, by trial and error, to teach her students how to include their processes as well as their computations in all mathematics work. This chapter is the culmination of her work on this genre. Her annotated model of a math response will help you conceptualize for your students all of the integral components expected in an exemplary mathematics response.

In Chapter 7, Rocha provides a unique frame for the reflective essay, which has been often assigned, but not taught as a specific genre. In this chapter, she carefully lays out a procedure for having students understand what a reflection is, what it looks like, and how an author portrays reflective thinking to an audience. Her audience selection chart is quite extensive and is one that you can use for just about any genre.

In Chapter 8, I offer a simple teaching event for expository summary writing. In this chapter, I suggest that writing summaries of expository text is a two-literacy event. First the reader must read and comprehend the text information followed by recording main ideas and composing a cohesive summary. The reading comprehension instructional strategies I present in this chapter are also helpful for teaching students to take notes for a research paper.

To extend your self-study of teaching genre by genre, the final chapter of this book is an annotated list of resources for teaching writing in the middle school. Included in the chapter are books, Web sites, videos, and resources for any content area.

Finally, as mentioned earlier, Appendix A includes rubrics for each genre presented in the book. Appendix B contains copy-friendly pages of all the figures included throughout this book. The material in this Appendix is designed for you to use in your own classroom. Feel free to utilize this section for student handouts and transparencies to support your instruction. Included in this Appendix are the model essays written to illustrate each genre, purpose and audience selection charts, and graphic organizers to help students select topics and outline their essays.

As you use the chapters in this book to enhance your teaching, feel free to experiment with the different teaching events presented in each chapter. Also, as your students begin their work producing writing genre by genre, be sure to keep exemplary essays to use as models for new students to read and examine. The chapter authors of this volume wrote the model essays, but all suggest that once you have generated student essays, use those to help other students conceptualize the genre. Also worthy of note is that all model essays included in this book are written using the Modern Language Association (Gibaldi, 2003) style.

Real teachers using teaching events from real middle school classrooms collaborated on this book. We hope it inspires you to experiment with genre writing instruction in your own classroom.

CHAPTER 2

THE NARRATIVE ACCOUNT

Beyond the Story

Michele M. Barlow and Melissa L. Francis

THE NATURE OF THE GENRE

When you write a narrative account, you are telling a story. And like any story, narrative accounts will include plots, settings, and characters, and incorporate use of dialogue and action in order to develop these story elements. A narrative account is also filled with details that are used to explain, support, and enhance the story for the reader (National Center on Education, 1997). The writer often evaluates the experiences and events described in the story, and explores the meaning of those experiences and events. The main purpose for writing narrative accounts is to inform and entertain. A good narrative account should include the following:

- an interesting lead that engages the reader
- a plot, setting, and characters
- a strong, identifiable story line
- a clear point of view (written in either first person or third person)
- an organized structure that has a beginning, middle, and end

Teaching Writing Genres Across the Curriculum, pages 15–31
Copyright © 2006 by Information Age Publishing

- concrete, vivid details to maintain the reader's attention
- specific narrative action such as dialogue, tension and/or suspense
- a conclusion that wraps up the story and suggests a consequence

A narrative account could tell either of the following:

1. The story of an actual experience that happened to the writer or another real-life figure, such as an autobiography or a biography.
2. A fictional story that is grounded in reality such as historical fiction, a fictionalized biography, or science fiction.

Some examples of narrative writing prompts for middle school content areas include:

Social Studies

- Tell a story about an important historical event to which you were an eyewitness.
- Choose a part of the world where you've never lived. Create a story about one day in your life. Embed what you know of the culture into your story.
- Write a story, which takes place during a specific time and place in history (e.g., the American Revolution, the sinking of the Titanic).

Mathematics

Imagine you are _____, a famous mathematician. Write an account about the events that led up to your discovery of _____.

Science and Technology

- Imagine yourself as a _____ (insert an inanimate object, animal, or plant). Describe what a typical day would be like for you.
- You go to sleep on July 4, 2006. You wake up July 4, 2056. Write an account of what life is like 50 years in the future. Ground your story in projections about future technological advances.
- Imagine you are _____, the famous inventor. Tell the story about the day you created your popular invention.

Health

- Write an account based on a strange news story about a widespread illness affecting your school.
- Place yourself in the middle of the plague years of the 1700s. Tell a story about the events before, during, or after the plague affected your town.

English

- Find an old photograph. Write a story based on the scene.
- Write the story that led to a turning point in your life.

Writing narrative accounts is a unique and creative way for students to exhibit their knowledge about a particular content area topic and to express their own point of view on the topic.

Now that you have a good understanding of the purpose for writing narrative accounts and the various elements that shape this genre, you are ready to begin teaching your students the steps involved in writing an exceptional narrative account.

How often have you been told that students learn best when they are actively involved in a new task? Well, that is absolutely true, especially when creating a quality piece of writing. As you recall from Chapter 1, writing is a *process*, not just a means to an end. Hence, learning to write a particular genre (in this case, a narrative account) cannot be successfully completed without learning how to accomplish each step of the process. The steps illustrated in this chapter will allow you to clearly model for your students how to write a narrative account in the content areas from the planning stage to the publishing stage. As stated earlier, teaching by means of active involvement is more powerful than any other style of teaching. So, before you ask your students to write their own narrative accounts, it is essential that you model the entire process first and have the students assist you at every step.

INTRODUCING THE GENRE: USING A MODEL ESSAY TO EXEMPLIFY THE GENRE

First, you must present a well-written narrative account, which will be used to introduce your students to the genre. The narrative should be age-appropriate for middle school students in both style and content, and possess all the elements characteristic of this type of genre. You may choose to write your own narrative account or use the model essay below.

Once you have chosen an exemplary narrative account, read it to your students while they listen. Following is a narrative account that took place during the American Revolution. You will notice that historical information is embedded throughout the story.

Model Essay: The Knock on the Door

The loud thud jolted Samuel out of his chair. He spun his head around and looked at the front door. "It's just the wind, Samuel," said his mother, Mary. "Now please sit down and finish your arithmetic before that candle burns out."

"Yes, Ma," Samuel sighed.

He sat down to finish his work, but he just couldn't concentrate. The wind had been pounding the old door all night. His father, John, had meant to fix its hinges, but he never got around to it.

Five months earlier, in the spring of 1780, Samuel's father had left home to fight with the American Army under the command of General Nathaniel Greene (White 3). He was supposed to be somewhere in North Carolina at the moment helping to chase the British Army north. America had been at war with England for over five years in an attempt to win its independence. Much of the fighting between 1778 and 1780 took place in the South, where the British Army had control over many regions (White 3). Samuel and his mother prayed every night for his father's safe return to their tiny farm in Williamsburg County, South Carolina. The day he left, John told Samuel to look after his mother and help her tend to the farm. He also told Samuel to make him proud. Samuel didn't quite understand what the word *proud* meant, but he never bothered to ask his father as he hugged him tight and said, "Goodbye."

As Samuel finished his last arithmetic problem, there was another loud rattle against the door. "I know, I know…it's just the wind," Samuel said, as he turned to kiss his mother goodnight.

BOOM! BOOM! BOOM!

The sound made the hair on Samuel's neck stand up. "Someone's at the door!" he yelled. Mary rose from her chair and whispered to Samuel, "Go up to the loft and hide under your bed. Don't come out until I say so." Samuel nodded and quickly hopped up the ladder to the loft. Meanwhile, Mary picked up a loose floorboard and gently pulled out a long, slim, gray musket. She had not yet needed to use it, but she knew that the person on the other side of the door could be a British soldier looking for food, or a place to sleep…or worse.

BOOM! BOOM! BOOM!

Samuel could feel his heart beating in his chest as Mary slowly released the latch on the door and stepped back, pointing the musket straight ahead. The door flew open and a tall figure stumbled to the floor. Mary dropped the musket and called out, "Samuel, come down here quickly! This man is badly hurt! Help me get him into the house!" Samuel ran toward his mother and the man lying on the floor. There was dark red blood all over the man's clothes and he was moaning loudly, like an injured animal. As Samuel and his mother pulled the man inside, Samuel's eyes widened in horror. The man's jacket was red!

"Ma, he's a Redcoat!" Samuel screamed.

"Never mind that now, Samuel!" Mary shouted back. "Just get me some clean rags and a bucket of fresh water."

Samuel didn't move. He couldn't. He just stood there, his eyes frozen on the enemy lying on the floor in a small pool of blood. Mary told Samuel to go upstairs and wait for her until she was finished. She found the wound on the soldier's right shoulder, and cleaned it with water. Then she poured homemade ointment on the wound and tied a butterfly bandage around it. The soldier looked into Mary's eyes, moaned softly, and then passed out.

The next morning, Samuel awoke to find his mother feeding the soldier a bowl of porridge. He never remembered falling asleep. The last thing he remembered was watching his mother wash the blood off the floor while the soldier rested next to the fire.

"Samuel," called his mother. "I want you to meet Thomas Cooke. He says he was hurt two days ago during a battle at Kings Mountain, just north of here" (White 3). Samuel just stared down at his feet. He didn't really care. He only wanted to know one thing. "Have you ever killed anyone?" he asked in a whisper.

"Yes, I'm afraid I have young man," replied Thomas. He continued to speak. "I want you to know that I am truly grateful for your mother's kindness, and as soon as I am feeling better, I will be on my way." Samuel nodded without looking at the soldier, and then walked into the kitchen. He appeared a few minutes later with a butter sandwich in his hand and offered it to the soldier. "Thank you very much, young man," Thomas said with a smile. "You're welcome," Samuel muttered back.

For the next three days, Samuel spent a lot of time with Thomas. He learned that Thomas had a son named Jacob, who was the same age as Samuel, living at home with his mother in England. Thomas showed Samuel how to play a new game with his marbles, and even helped him with his arithmetic. Samuel almost forgot that Thomas was an enemy soldier. But then the day came when Thomas had to leave.

"I'll always remember your kindness, Mary," Thomas said softly. He put his hand on Samuel's shoulder, "And I cannot wait to tell my son all about you, Samuel."

"Goodbye, Thomas," said Samuel.

As Thomas walked away with his musket in hand, Samuel looked at his mother. She knew that he didn't understand why Thomas had to go back and fight. "Your father would be very proud of you right now, Samuel," she said. Samuel now understood what that word meant.

WORKS CITED

White, D. The American Revolutionary War: Keeping Independence, Part 3: The End and the Beginning. January 29, 2005. Social Studies for Kids. Available at: http://www.socialstudiesforkids.com/articles/ushistory/revolutionarywar3.htm

Elements of the Genre

After reading the story, place a transparency of the account on an overhead projector, give each student a copy, and read the story again; this time asking students to focus on the elements of the genre and the characteristics that make the narrative account an exemplary piece of writing that holds the readers' interest. Refer to Figure 2.1 to help you with this step. (Note: Appendix B contains full-size figures you can reproduce to make handouts and transparencies for your class.)

Students' responses may reveal that the first few sentences grab their attention, or that the narrator makes them feel as if they are part of the story. This particular activity can also be conducted in small groups and then shared with the entire class. You may need to read the narrative account several times in order to assist your students in identifying all of the elements present. At the end of this step, you should impress upon your students that the narrative account is essentially a story that relies on vivid factual details to describe the characters and events and allows readers to experience the story.

Elements of a Narrative Account

Lead	The lead is the first sentence of the piece. It attracts the reader to read on.
Sensory Details	Use of sensory details (sight, sound, taste, touch, and smell) makes the story feel as real as possible.
Story Structure	A narrative account is a story woven around factual information, and has a setting, characters, and events that lead up to a climax and a strong conclusion.
Storyline	A narrative account should have a strong storyline with specific narrative action such as dialogue, tension and/or suspense.
Author's Style	A narrative account has a strong author's voice and vivid word choice.
Point of View	A narrative account is either written in first or third person.
Conclusion	The conclusion wraps up the story and suggests a consequence.

Figure 2.1.   Elements of a narrative account.

PLANNING STEP 1: SELECTING A TOPIC FOR THE NARRATIVE ACCOUNT

Once your students have a clear understanding of the elements that shape a narrative account, you are now ready to model how to select a topic. Since the main purpose of a narrative account is to entertain the reader and stimulate his emotions, you need to ensure that your students are able to do the following: (a) select a person or event they find interesting and, therefore, worth writing about, and (b) gather enough details about the person or event to make the account real for the reader.

If you are a content area teacher, you may want to have your students write narrative accounts based on topics studied in class. For example, a social studies teacher may have his students write a fictional account as eyewitnesses to a historical event. A science teacher, on the other hand, may have his students imagine they are a piece of food and write a fictional account relating their experiences as they travel through the human digestive system. In either case, the process your students will follow in order to select their topics is the same. The individual steps involved in deciding on a topic are as follows:

1. Draw a circle in the middle of a blank piece of paper and write the name of your general topic inside the circle. (As stated earlier, content area teachers will likely decide on the general topic their students will write about based on a current, or past, unit of study.)

2. Brainstorm all of the experiences and knowledge you have associated with the general topic. For each idea you brainstorm, create a semantic web (use only simple words and phrases). This is called a *broad topic web*. See Figure 2.2 for a broad topic selection web based on the model essay.

3. As you can see in Figure 2.2, the information in the web is still very general. It would be very difficult for your students, at this point, to begin writing their narrative accounts with so many areas on which to focus. Therefore, one idea from the broad topic web must be chosen (based on interest level) and developed further.

4. As you continue to model, write the idea chosen from your broad topic web in the center of a new piece of paper. Draw a circle around the idea.

5. Brainstorm all of the experiences and knowledge you have associated with the idea, developing a story line as you go along. You may need to gather additional information from other sources, such as textbooks, journals, and the Internet. In order to make your modeling as interesting and authentic as possible, you must brainstorm many story details regarding the setting, plot, and characters that will eventually support and enhance your story. This is called a *narrow topic web*. See Figure 2.3 for a narrow topic selection web based on the model essay.

6. Ask students to try selecting their own topics using the technique you just modeled. Have students talk to peers during this process to set the tone for a writer's workshop that includes sharing ideas.

7. If your students are unable to collect at least 8–10 story details, then you must refer them back to their broad topic webs and encourage them to choose another idea to develop.

8. Once students have chosen a story line for which they can generate many story details, they now have a worthwhile topic for their narrative accounts.

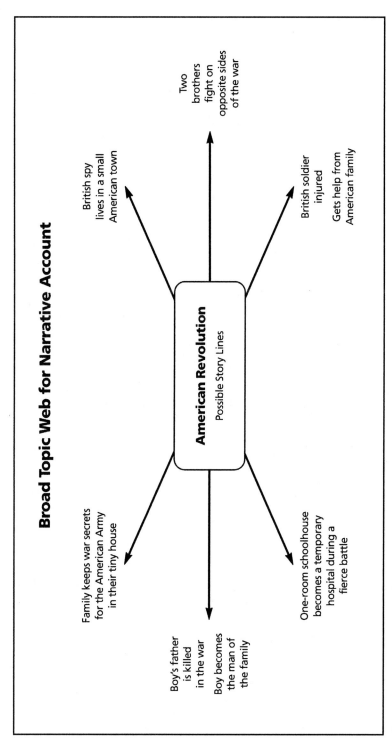

Figure 2.2. Broad topic web for narrative account.

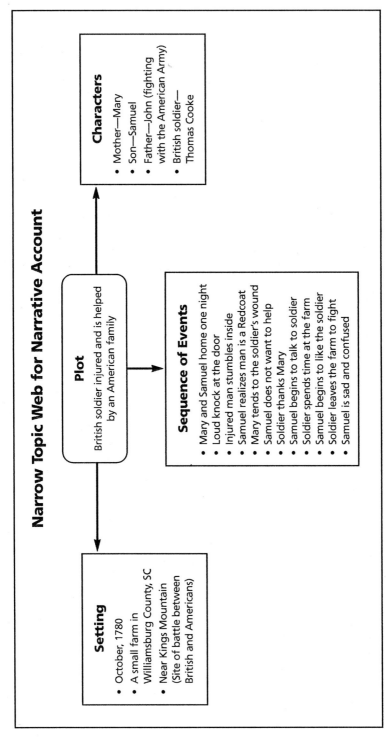

Figure 2.3. Narrow topic web for narrative account.

PLANNING STEP 2: SELECTING AN AUDIENCE

Once your students understand how to narrow ideas in order to select a topic to write about, you are ready to demonstrate how to select the audience who will read their narrative accounts. Having the students understand their audience before they begin writing will allow them to accomplish the following: (a) clearly identify their purpose for writing, (b) choose how simple (or complex) the language should be, and (c) determine how much description they will need to provide. If all three of these areas are addressed when the students begin writing, their final pieces will ensure audience engagement.

Perhaps one of the simplest approaches to selecting an audience is to have your students work through the questioning suggested in Figure 2.4. You can model for students how to select an audience using the model essay they read earlier.

Determine the Audience for Your Narrative Account

In order to make writing your narrative account easier, complete the three statements below. Then keep this sheet next to you when you begin writing to help you determine your choice of language and how much description you need to provide your reader.

Why are you writing this account?
I am writing this account to... (check the phrase(s) that apply):
- ☐ explain something.
- ☐ entertain.
- ☐ share a personal story.
- ☐ narrate a story as an eyewitness to a historical event.
- ☐ describe a historical or scientific event from a character's point of view.
- ☐ tell an original tale.
- ☐ make readers feel good.

For whom are you writing this account?
I am writing this account for... (check the phrase(s) that apply):
- ☐ younger children (specify age group: _____).
- ☐ my peers (specify: _____).
- ☐ older children (specify age group: _____).
- ☐ my parents.
- ☐ other family members (specify: _____).
- ☐ the general public (specify: _____).

How much does your audience know about your topic?
My audience is... (check the phrase that applies)
- ☐ not familiar with my topic.
- ☐ somewhat familiar with my topic.
- ☐ very familiar with my topic.

Figure 2.4.   Audience selection for narrative account.

PLANNING STEP 3: BRAINSTORMING, RECORDING, AND ORGANIZING INFORMATION

After your students collect their information, they must learn how to organize it with the use of a graphic organizer. A graphic organizer is an instructional tool used to illustrate a student's knowledge about a topic.

For this step, we suggest you place a transparency of the graphic organizer shown in Figure 2.5 on an overhead projector and give each student a copy.

Discuss each section of the graphic organizer and what type of information should be included. Next, place a transparency of the graphic organizer without the text on an overhead projector and demonstrate how to fill it in using the information gathered in your narrow topic web. There is no need to use complete sentences when you model this step. Words and phrases are appropriate.

This particular step is a difficult one for students to master, especially if they have had little or no experience using graphic organizers. Therefore, make sure that your students are comfortable using this graphic organizer before moving on to the next step.

COMPOSING THE ROUGH DRAFT

So far, all of the planning involved in writing the narrative account has been conducted in bits and pieces. It is now time to model for your students how to put those bits and pieces together to create a first draft. Each section of the graphic organizer can be translated into a paragraph in order to create a strong beginning, middle, and end of a story. Demonstrate for your students how to use sequence words and transitions to connect the paragraphs in a fluent manner.

REVISING THE ROUGH DRAFT

Good writing requires revision. Revision means looking at your written work again and making necessary changes. Writers usually need to revise a piece of writing more than once until it is "finished."

Once you have created a working copy of your narrative account, you can now model how you will enhance the story to capture and hold the readers' interest. Two of the most important elements of a good narrative account are the author's ability to capture his readers' attention in the first few sentences and his use of sensory details (sight, sound, taste, touch, and

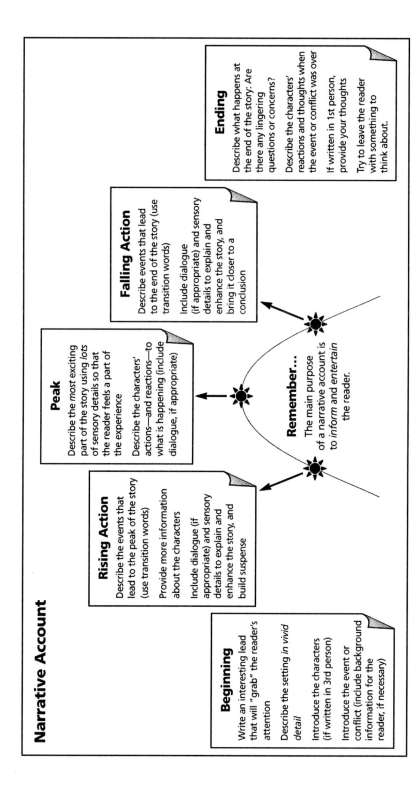

Figure 2.5. Graphic organizer for narrative account.

Narrative Account

Beginning

Write an interesting lead that will "grab" the reader's attention

Describe the setting *in vivid detail*

Introduce the characters (if written in 3rd person)

Introduce the event or conflict (include background information for the reader, if necessary)

Rising Action

Describe the events that lead to the peak of the story (use transition words)

Provide more information about the characters

Include dialogue (if appropriate) and sensory details to explain and enhance the story, and build suspense

Peak

Describe the *most exciting* part of the story using *lots* of sensory details so that the reader feels a part of the experience

Describe the characters' actions—and reactions—to what is happening (include dialogue, if appropriate)

Falling Action

Describe events that lead to the end of the story (use transition words)

Include dialogue (if appropriate) and sensory details to explain and enhance the story, and bring it closer to a conclusion

Ending

Describe what happens at the end of the story: Are there any lingering questions or concerns?

Describe the characters' reactions and thoughts when the event or conflict was over

If written in 1st person, provide your thoughts

Try to leave the reader with something to think about.

Remember...

The main purpose of a narrative account is to *inform* and *entertain* the reader.

smell) to make the story feel as real as possible. You will likely need to teach your students how to incorporate each of these elements into their narrative accounts during the revision process.

For example, in order to teach students how to create sensory details, have them make a chart similar to the one below. Next, tell your students to list each major event from their accounts in the left column. For each event, ask your students to imagine the sights, sounds, smells, tastes, and textures important to their stories. Then tell them to list the words that come to mind as they visualize these events in the middle column. Lastly, ask your students to list the emotions they or their characters felt during each event.

Events	Sensory Details	Emotions

After students have created their charts, ask them to go back to their stories and see if each event can be embellished with these sensory details and emotions. We found that asking students to add sensory details and enhance descriptions is a revision process that they enjoy.

Obtain Feedback through Teacher and Peer Conferences

Once the draft has been revised at least once, it is time to show it to another person in order to obtain audience feedback. As the teacher, you should conduct individual writing conferences with your students. The writing conference is a very valuable tool to observe, assess, and evaluate the individual writing development of your students (Graves, 1983). As you hold individual writing conferences with your students, have the genre rubric present so that specific areas of the narrative account can be addressed and discussed.

One good way to give students practice in both reading and writing is to have them take part in peer review. Peer review involves students reading each other's works and then providing constructive feedback. It should be noted, however, that students are often uneasy at first with the notion of peer review because they are afraid to provide constructive criticism to their peers *and* have their own work examined. To avoid these pitfalls, you should model how to provide the most helpful kinds of responses and make good use of the feedback received. Figure 2.6 can be used specifically for giving and receiving feedback on narrative accounts.

Peer Feedback Form
(Narrative Account)

Presenter: _____

Title: _____

TWO PAIRS OF EYES ARE BETTER THAN ONE!

Read my story carefully. When you are finished, please take the time to complete the chart and answer the questions below as thoroughly as you can. Be honest! Your responses will help make my story better. Thank you.

	Needs Improvement	Good	Excellent
The lead captures my attention.			
The story held my interest.			
I feel a part of the experience described in the story.			
The story is clear and organized.			

What did you like **best** about the story?

Describe how I can **improve** the story.

Reviewer's Name: _____   **Date:** _____

Figure 2.6.   Peer review feedback form for narrative account.

EDITING THE ROUGH DRAFT

The content and style of the narrative account is now in place. However, you now need to model for your students how to edit their written work so that any errors in language usage and spelling that remain are corrected. Set aside time to conduct a few short lessons on specific editing strategies (Weaver, 1996). The writing conferences you hold will enable you to determine which editing strategies your students need to learn.

Also, during the final editing stages, it is helpful to demonstrate how to proofread writing pieces. Tell your students to read their stories out loud and *s-l-o-w-l-y*, so that they can both see *and* hear their own words. This method will help the students detect any mistakes in language usage and spelling.

PUBLISHING THE FINAL DRAFT

The revised and edited draft is ready to be put into its final form (either handwritten or typed). In addition to the final copy, you may ask your students to prepare a title page, number the pages of their stories, and include illustrations, diagrams, or charts if appropriate. If your students have used books to gather information, you will need to teach them how to cite these books using Modern Language Association (MLA) documentation (Gibaldi, 2003).

Finally, don't forget to ask your students to give you all of the forms and drafts they completed, so that you can measure their growth throughout the writing process and ensure that each step of the writing process was followed.

SHARING THE FINAL DRAFT

Congratulations! Your students are ready to share their narrative accounts with an audience. Do not skip this step! The main purpose for writing is to communicate one's thoughts with others. When students are given the opportunity to share their writing with others, they feel a true sense of satisfaction for a job well done!

EVALUATING THE FINAL DRAFT

Included in the Appendix is an evaluation rubric for the narrative account. The rubric has three purposes. First, it provides your students with clear descriptions of what good performance looks like as they begin to write their narrative accounts. Second, it provides you with a more precise and objective means of assessing your students' written work—one that is consistent and fair. Third, it provides your students with clear information about how well they performed and what they need to accomplish in the future to improve their performance.

In order to give your students the ability to produce an exemplary narrative account, you should introduce the rubric during the planning stages of the writing process. Begin by sharing the rubric with your students after the model essay has been read and the elements of the genre have been identified. As you read through the rubric, it is essential that your students understand the rubric language. If any language is difficult to comprehend, allow your students to change it so that all students have a clear understanding of the criteria. Next, have your students assist you as you evaluate the model narrative account using the rubric. You may want to evaluate other narrative accounts that represent a range of performance so that your students understand what an "exemplary" narrative account looks like versus what an "acceptable" narrative account looks like.

After the rubric has been introduced and shared with the class, give each student a copy of the rubric so that he/she may refer to it during the writing process. During writing conferences, ask students to reference the rubric to determine what they need to do in order to improve the writing piece.

Once your students produce their final drafts, you may then use the rubric as your evaluation tool. Your final evaluation results will also give you an indication of what area(s) you may need to teach more thoroughly in the future.

CHAPTER 3

THE PERSUASIVE ESSAY

Students' Opinions on Controversial Topics

Megan L. Labrecque and Tara A. Fernandes

THE NATURE OF THE GENRE

What is a persuasive essay? A persuasive essay is a way for students to persuade their readers to consider their opinions. The purpose of persuasive writing is to identify a stance on a particular issue and to attempt to sway readers' thinking on a given topic (National Center on Education, 1997).

The primary focus of persuasive writing is to persuade readers, but a secondary focus can be to inform. Regardless of the topic, your students' opinions will need to be supported by factual information. Whether or not the primary goal of convincing the reader to agree with an opinion is accomplished, the reader will have learned something about the issue that your students are addressing.

Persuasive writing can be used in a variety of content areas, including science, social studies, literature, and/or current events. For example, your students can use persuasive writing to try to convince your school principal that a school dress code is unnecessary, attempt to get a group of smokers to quit, or to help save the environment by informing the readers of the hazards of littering.

Teaching Writing Genres Across the Curriculum, pages 33–48
Copyright © 2006 by Information Age Publishing
All rights of reproduction in any form reserved.

By participating in this genre study, students will be able to accomplish the following:

1. Learn the steps that make up the process of writing a persuasive essay.
2. Research reasons and factual evidence to support their opinions and state them in a clear, direct manner.
3. Gain confidence in expressing their ideas and theories.

INTRODUCING THE GENRE: USING A MODEL ESSAY TO EXEMPLIFY THE GENRE

In order to get started, we suggest that you have your students understand what it means to "be persuasive." A simple method is to make a web with the word "persuade" in the center. Ask students to brainstorm what that word means to them. Record their responses and ask structured questions to bring them to a satisfactory conclusion of what it means "to persuade."

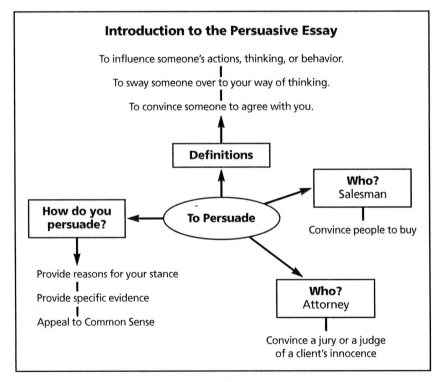

Figure 3.1.   Persuasive essay definition web.

Additionally, you can ask students to think of people who are naturally persuasive (such as attorneys and salespeople) and to consider their persuasive techniques. Conclude this step by asking students to generate ideas about what they do when they want to persuade their parents or friends. Figure 3.1 is an example of a "hopeful" finished web. (Note: Appendix B contains full-size figures you can reproduce to make handouts and transparencies for your class.)

Next, in order for students to understand what a persuasive essay looks like, you can have them read (aloud or silently) a model essay from your own archives or use the environmental science model essay provided below. As students read, have them think about characteristics that make the piece persuasive. Following is a model essay you can use to accomplish this goal.

Model Essay: Littering: Not Just an Environmental Hazard!

Littering has been an ongoing problem in our society. Every year, the Environmental Protection Agency educates the general public through various forms of media on environmental hazards ("Trash" 5). Littering is one of them. Although education is provided on a consistent basis, littering continues to be a tremendous problem, affecting the environment, and many other aspects of our lives. Do you feel littering is a problem? Do you feel that littering affects wildlife? Do you feel that littering can be harmful to humans? Do you think littering is economically harmful? I do.

Litter does in fact affect wildlife. Animals can be harmed by the trash that people dispose of improperly. For example, the plastic rings on a six-pack of soda could kill a bird. People go on picnics to the park and beach and think nothing of bringing some soda to drink. Unfortunately, what people may not think of is that when they leave the plastic ring from the soda on the ground, a bird could mistake it for food. If a bird puts one of these in its mouth, it could get its beak tangled or even strangle itself. This is only one small example of how litter affects wildlife ("Trash" 3).

Littering can also be harmful to humans. Many people do not realize that when they are littering, there is a good chance they could be harming themselves in the process. Often, beaches can be forced to close at times during the summer due to water pollution levels and litter being too unsafe for swimmers. "Beach users can be injured by stepping on broken glass, cans, needles or other litter" ("Trash" 3). Are you one of those people who have visited the first aid station because you were barefoot on a beach and were cut on a broken soda bottle? This is a direct consequence of people littering. In addition, people can get sick from drinking contaminated water. Contaminated water could be the result of harmful chemicals, from your litter, absorbing into the ground. Is your drinking water safe?

Lastly, litter is economically harmful. When someone throws a piece of trash on the ground rather than in a receptacle, they are probably not thinking about how much it will cost to be picked up. According to the state of Georgia Department of Transportation ("The Dirty Facts" 1), 15 million dollars has been spent to clean up highway litter in one year. According to the Environmental Protection Agency: "New Jersey spends 1.5 million dollars annually to clean up its beaches" ("Trash" 3). In summary, each year, millions of dollars are spent to clean up after careless people who improperly dispose of their trash. With the economy struggling as it is, money should not have to be used for something that can be prevented.

In conclusion, is littering a problem? Does littering harm wildlife, humans, and the economy? Yes, littering can be harmful; however there are many solutions as to where to dispose trash rather than to turn it into litter. People need to be more educated and less careless. Everyone needs to do his or her part in helping clean up. If you see a piece of trash on the ground, you should bring it to a trash receptacle. If everyone did what he or she could to reduce litter, it wouldn't be such a harmful and expensive problem!

WORKS CITED

Trash In Our Oceans. 2 Feb. 2005. Environmental Protection Agency. 5 Feb. 2005. Available at: http://www.epa.gov/owow/oceans/debris/index.html

The Dirty Facts: Litter in Georgia. 26 Sept. 2003. Georgia Department of Transportation. 3 Feb. 2005. Available at: http://www.stoplittering.com.

Elements of the Genre

As described in Chapter 1, identifying the elements of the genre is essential to having students understand the nature of the piece. Once the model essay has been read, you can position students to think critically about the elements of a persuasive essay by asking: "What makes this littering essay persuasive?" As students respond, record their responses on the board or on a blank overhead transparency. To be sure you have generated all of the genre elements, you can add to the students' list by consulting the elements suggested in Figure 3.2.

Elements of a Persuasive Essay

- The piece has a clear purpose: to persuade the audience to agree.
- The piece addresses a consistent audience.
- The opinion is clearly stated in the opening paragraph.
- Established facts and/or opinions are provided as reasons for the argument.
- Reasons for writer's stance are supported with reasons and evidence so that the reader better understands the issue.
- Background knowledge is provided for those who do not know about the topic.
- Strong persuasive words appropriate to the audience are used.
- The piece includes a conclusion that restates the main ideas and briefly reflects on the importance of the argument.

Figure 3.2.   Elements of a good persuasive essay.

PLANNING STEP 1: SELECTING A TOPIC FOR THE PERSUASIVE ESSAY

Teaching Students to Select an Initial Topic

To select a topic, begin by presenting your students with a broad subject of interest in your content area. The grid below suggests content area topics suitable for a persuasive essay.

Science	Social Studies	Community	Health
Amphibians	Issues in China	Dress codes	Weight loss
Cloning	Slavery	School policies	Exercise
Environmental concerns	American revolution	School budgets	Food pyramids

You can choose any broad topic that is vital to your current curriculum and model for students how to write that topic in the center of a piece of paper. As you model, create a semantic map and expand upon the subject or topic by thinking aloud about the expansion of the topic.

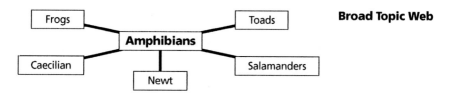

Teaching Students to Narrow an Initial Topic

Now, ask students to choose only one of the expanded topics. Have the students make the expanded topic more specific by using the 5 Ws (Who, What, When, Where, and Why) that are specific to that topic.

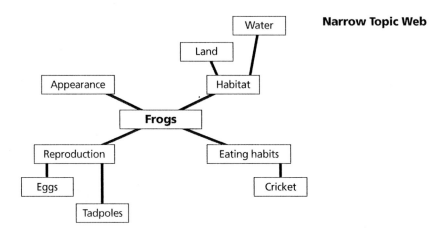

Narrow Topic Web

Generating Questions to Focus Purpose of Essay

Looking at the specific topics the students generated, ask them to choose one narrow topic and try to formulate a question that has a pro or con. For example:

TOPIC—Frog Habitat

FORMULATED QUESTION—Can frogs live in areas without water?

Point out to students that they must be able to defend the specific topic of choice and persuade their readers to take sides. Therefore, if the students are unable to formulate a question for their topic then maybe that topic is not the best choice. Encourage students to keep on trying to formulate a question until they have generated a focus question they can defend.

We have found that generating focus questions for the persuasive essay is actually easier for students if your broad topic choice has a built-in issue such as the benefits or drawbacks of stem cell research or cloning. We chose to present the amphibian example in this chapter so you could see that almost any topic can be used successfully for the persuasive genre. During this step, it is important that as a final outcome, students have turned their topics into focus questions.

PLANNING STEP 2: SELECTING AN AUDIENCE
AND PURPOSE FOR WRITING

Now that your students have chosen their topics and formulated a question to defend, they need to think about their audience and their purpose for writing. What is the purpose of the piece? Are they hoping their audience will consider their argument or be persuaded about an issue or topic? For whom are they writing? Novices or experts in the field? Friends, family, or outsiders?

As described in Chapter 1, students need to think about these questions to plan both the level of detail and the amount of description needed in their pieces. Figure 3.3 will help you to model this step for your students. Your goal is to have students understand the importance of their purpose and audience selection. After you model, have students work in pairs to help select their target audience and declare the purpose for the writing piece.

Determining a Purpose and Selecting an Audience
for your Persuasive Essay

1. **What is my *purpose*? Am I trying to:**
   - ☐ Inform my readers of things they may not know?
   - ☐ Convince my readers of my point of view?
   - ☐ Bring about change in my readers' thinking? Persuade?
   - ☐ Challenge my readers' thinking about my point of view?

2. Who is my *audience?*
   - ☐ Friends?
   - ☐ Students?
   - ☐ Teachers?
   - ☐ Parents?
   - ☐ Others?

3. **What type of word choice should I use for this type of audience?**

4. **How hard do I have to work to convince my audience of my point of view?**
   - ☐ Will they join my side? Will they agree with me? Will they change their opinions?
   - ☐ Will they think about what I wrote?
   - ☐ Will they consider a new point of view?

Figure 3.3.   Purpose and audience selection for the persuasive essay.

PLANNING STEP 3: FORMULATING A LEAD

A good lead sentence grabs the reader's attention. In a persuasive piece of writing, the lead may be the question students have already determined earlier or it may just be introductory information. In either case, the lead will need to spark debate in order to introduce the reader's stance on the issue as well as to get the reader thinking. To formulate a good lead sentence, or opening question, students will need to consider the following:

- What is the issue I am trying to address?
- What are both sides of the issue?
- What is my stance on this particular issue?
- How do I want the reader to know what my stance on the issue is?
- How do I want the reader to feel about this particular issue?
- How can I "grab" my readers' attention?

For example, in our littering essay we used a simple statement as the lead:

"Littering has been an ongoing problem in our society."

We felt it was more compelling than to use our generated focus question:

"Do you feel littering is a problem?"

Either way, we found that it is important for students to think about their leads before they go about researching and recording facts. By articulating the lead up front, we believe it helps students to once again consider the purpose of the essay. We suggest you model for them alternate leads for the littering essay using the questions bulleted above to help guide your think aloud.

Explain to your students that you are asking them to think about their leads now, but they may want to revise them later on in the writing process. Again, the purpose of having students consider their leads now is to focus their essay on one single purpose.

PLANNING STEP 4: BRAINSTORMING REASONS AND RESEARCHING FACTUAL EVIDENCE

When looking back at our model essay, you will see how our reasons and factual evidence were presented in an organized way. However, you may be surprised that the actual preliminary organizing began at this step. Below is an example of a chart what we made at the conclusion of our brainstorming and research.

Reasons	Possible Evidence	More Specific Evidence
Reason 1. Littering affects wildlife	1. Plastic soda rings 2. Animals harmed 3. Birds can mistake for food	1. Left at parks and beaches 3. Get their beaks tangled or strangle themselves
Reason 2. Littering affects humans	1. Trash left on ground 2. Getting hurt 3. Contaminated water	2. Glass left at the beach 3. Harmful chemicals can leak into the ground
Reason 3. Littering costs money	1. Towns have to hire cleanup crews 2. Trash on roads 3. Money used for other things	1. Georgia's Department of Transportation spends about 11 million dollars per year on cleaning up trash on highways

When looking at this example, you will notice that the chart is broken down into two main sections: reasons and evidence. Using this example, we will take you through this two-step process of how to teach your students to formulate reasons and then conduct research to find factual evidence.

For the first step, the students will need to brainstorm three or more appropriate reasons for their stance that they would like the audience to consider in their piece. The students will need to remember to use the formulated question and the lead sentence, previously written, in order to keep the piece focused on their target audience and their stance. By taking part in this first step, it allows the students to be more focused on the specific evidence that they will need to support their reasons.

In addition to brainstorming their reasons, we also have the students brainstorm possible evidence before consulting research sources. Below is an example of our chart at the conclusion of this step in the process.

Reasons	Possible Evidence	More Specific Evidence
Reason 1. Littering affects wildlife	1. Plastic soda rings 2. 3.	
Reason 2. Littering affects humans	1. Contaminated water 2. 3.	
Reason 3. Littering costs money	1. Towns have to hire cleanup crews 2. 3.	

If the students have not previously learned how to gather facts, take notes, and cite information for a research paper, you may need to provide a lesson now. As a reference, Chapter 4 of this volume (Figure 4.4) has a standard note-sheet format that we find useful as students gather information from sources.

The second step, researching, asks the students to look for evidence to support the reasons brainstormed earlier and these should be logged in the possible evidence column. If evidence cannot be found to support their reasons, they may have to develop an alternate reason. Please remember to explain to the students that as they research, this information may change. They may find a more compelling reason in source material that they should note under the reason column or they may find superior supportive evidence that should be noted in the more specific evidence column. The target goal for the students, when the research is done, should be to find three reasons that support their stance with three pieces of evidence for each reason.

PLANNING STEP 5: ORGANIZING INFORMATION

Now that your students have seen an example of a persuasive essay, chosen a topic and an audience, and researched their facts, they must organize the information in a manner that will produce a well-organized essay.

We have provided a model graphic organizer (see Figure 3.4) based on the "littering" essay presented earlier in this chapter to help you model this step for your students. Since this is a difficult step in the process, we have included a set of clear directions for modeling the recording of information onto the graphic organizer. You may want to consider modeling this part of the essay *while* your students are researching and collecting information for their essays because it is important that they *truly* understand that a persuasive essay has clear parts of information gathering: reasons for their argument and supporting evidence.

Model Recording the Main Ideas for the Introduction of the Essay

Using the introduction from the model essay, model for your students how to begin their essay with a lead sentence in order to grab the audience's attention. You can place Figure 3.4, the unrecorded graphic organizer, on an overhead transparency and record the information as follows.

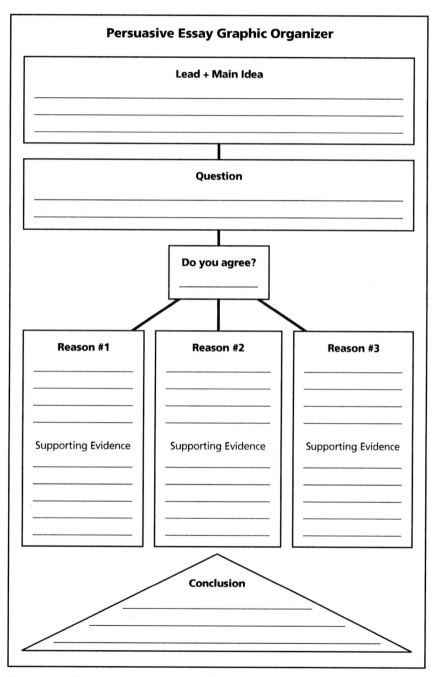

Figure 3.4.   Persuasive essay final planning organizer.

For example:

> **LEAD + MAIN IDEA**
> Littering has been an ongoing problem in our society. Every year, the Environmental Protection Agency educates the general public through various forms of media on environmental hazards (Trash 5). Littering is one of them. Although education is provided on a consistent basis, littering continues to be a tremendous problem, affecting the environment, and many other aspects of our lives.

For example: Using the topic of littering, the question that we constructed is:

> **QUESTION**
> Do you feel littering is a problem?

Now have your students decide whether or not they agree with the question that they constructed.
For example:

> **DO YOU AGREE?**
> Yes

Next, show students how to insert their question into the graphic organizer.

Model Recording the Main Ideas for the Body of the Essay

In order to defend their stance, students must brainstorm or collect from their note cards three or more reasons as to why they agree or not. You can model using the model essay and then have students practice with their own essays. Tell them that they may need to search through their note cards or go back to source materials for a minimum of three reasons to defend their arguments. Remind students that the reasons must be supported with factual evidence later in the essay. If they are not able to support them, then they are *not* good reasons. These reasons should be recorded in the "reason" boxes of the organizer without further detail.

Model writing the three reasons from the original essay before continuing onto the next stage.

For example:

> **REASON #1**
> Littering affects wildlife

Next, for each reason that your students brainstormed in planning step four to support their arguments, they are to record the three pieces of evidence that they gathered from their research. At this stage, students need to explain to their audience why they, as writers, agree or disagree with the question that was originally posed at the beginning of the piece in the first paragraph. Please remind your students that the goal of writing this piece is to get the reader to agree with their positions. The graphic organizer you are completing as a model will now begin to look like this:

> **REASON #2**
> Littering can be harmful to humans
>
> Supporting Evidence
>
> - Trash is disposed of improperly.
> - Trash can leak harmful chemicals into the ground and damage drinking water supplies.
> - Broken glasses at beaches can hurt you.

Continue modeling until students understand what they need to do with their own material. While students are completing the reason/evidence sections of their graphics, they will need much peer and teacher support.

Model Recording the Main Ideas for the Conclusion of the Essay

Finally, to conclude the essay, model for students how to:

- restate their stance on the original question and whether they agree or not, as done in paragraph one.
- restate each of their reasons briefly without going into detail in order to remind their audience.
- end the paragraph with the conclusion summing up the point that they were trying to get across in their piece.

For example:

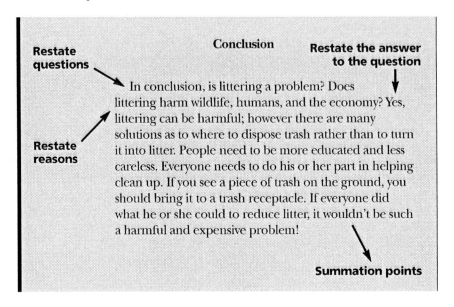

We have discovered that it is useful for students to switch graphic organizers with an able peer for feedback on the validity of their reasons and evidence. As a final check, it is wise for you to check each student's graphic organizer to be sure they have compelling reasons and direct evidence to support and defend their arguments.

COMPOSING THE ROUGH DRAFT

Once students have completed their graphics, you will notice that all main points have been identified plus the essay is already organized for the ease of drafting. We suggest you model for students how to use the graphic as a blue print to write a sequential rough draft. Point out that they should start a new paragraph for each reason. Once students understand the structure of the essay, you can have them try it out using their own graphic organizers.

REVISING AND EDITING THE ROUGH DRAFT

The revision and editing stages give students the opportunity to improve each draft of their piece. These processes, in addition to peer and teacher conferences, help students improve their pieces (Calkins, 1994; Graves, 1983; Weaver, 1996). As suggested in Chapter 1, generating a basic checklist can also be helpful for students during this process. We suggest the following steps for the revision and the editing process of the persuasive essay.

- Set the draft aside for at least 24 hours.
- Review all graphic organizers, notes, drafts, and rubrics.
- Think of ways to improve the draft by reading it aloud to a parent, friend, etc.
- Revise the draft paying attention to the strength of the argument.
- Confer with a peer to assist with revision.
- Self- edit the draft paying particular attention to sentence structure, subject-verb agreement, and punctuation.
- Confer with a peer to assist with editing.
- Review the piece with a teacher.
- Repeat revision and editing step as necessary.

PUBLISHING AND SHARING THE FINAL DRAFT

The publishing stage is the students' final step in which they prepare the piece for the target audience. Throughout this final process, students should prepare their pieces for display by typing the finished work including illustrations and/or diagrams if necessary. We suggest the following steps for the publishing process of the persuasive essay.

- Design a title page.
- Draw graphics and/or illustrations.
- Review the final copy for typographical errors.
- Review the final draft and check that all pages are included.

Finally, as suggested in Chapter 1, be sure to have your students take the author's chair (Calkins, 1994) and share their persuasive pieces with class-mates, family, and friends.

EVALUATING THE FINAL DRAFT

You will find an analytic evaluation rubric that we designed for the persuasive essay in Appendix A. We suggest that the evaluation rubric should be introduced when the genre task is first modeled in order for your students to evaluate their own work at each stage of the writing process. If you share how the rubric works with your students at the beginning of the genre study then they are aware of the criteria on which they will be graded and will work toward meeting the highest performance criteria.

When looking at the rubric, you will notice that one of the categories that the students are graded on is the writing process. *How accountable were they during the writing process? Did they keep their information organized in order to pass it in during this stage?* A second category is the content and the elements of the genre. *Did they follow the graphic organizer in order to formulate paragraphs that strongly persuade the reader? Did they listen to suggestions made during the student and teacher conference in order to improve the piece?* Grammar and mechanics is the third category. *Did the students use the tools within the classroom in order to fix their spelling, grammar, capitalization, and punctuation? Did they apply a new revision or editing strategy? Did they listen to suggestions made during the student and teacher conference in order to improve the piece?* Lastly, the style of the piece is investigated. *Did the student use vocabulary that was suitable for their audience? Do both the student and the reader understand the piece?*

Once students have finished their final drafts and self evaluated their pieces, you will be able to score the writing piece and help students identify the strengths and needs of their persuasive writing. When this step is completed, both teachers and students understand the rubric score as well as the improvements and strengths that can be applied in each student's next persuasive piece.

CHAPTER 4

THE FEATURE NEWSPAPER ARTICLE

More Than Just Facts

Suzanne K. Dunbar

THE NATURE OF THE GENRE

Feature newspaper articles present an exceptional format for middle school students to develop greater sophistication in their expository writing. When students enter middle school, it is expected that they can read for information, summarize main ideas, and produce a report of information (National Center on Education, 1997). A feature article builds on these essential skills and adds the component of perspective. While there is no single definition of this genre, a feature newspaper article presents factual information about people, places, events, or experiences and attempts to explain the topic from a specific point of view or perspective. As students research their topics, they must not only gather information, but also examine it critically to look for the big ideas and to develop "an angle" for presentation. Since the writer personalizes information and presents it through his or her perspective, feature articles allow the reader to view information in a new or different way.

In addition to developing depth, feature articles provide numerous opportunities for students to make choices in their writing, a factor that middle school students value. This genre can be used in any content area, as well as beyond the classroom for school newspapers or other publications. Students can explore topics in science, social studies, math, or health, or they can investigate an issue involving their school or community.

During the research process students can gather information from traditional sources, such as books, encyclopedias, or the Internet, or they might choose alternative sources including interviews, public documents, or surveys. Once they have collected their information, students must decide on an angle, choose an organizing structure to present information, and add supporting text features. As students go through the writing process, they become experts on their topics, and must also determine the most effective way of communicating their information.

Middle school teachers face an important task. They must transition students by building on the foundational skills learned in the elementary years and prepare them for the demands of high school writing. Feature newspaper articles provide a creative format for students to demonstrate their knowledge and strengthen their expository writing skills.

INTRODUCING THE GENRE: USING A MODEL ESSAY TO EXEMPLIFY THE GENRE

As suggested in Chapter 1 of this volume, in order for students to prepare to write a feature article, they must have an idea of the nature of the genre. To introduce students to the genre, you can use feature articles from newspapers as models of the genre or you can use the one included on the next page.

Before you introduce the models, take a few moments to brainstorm with students what they know about the genre. Ask them to consider what they would expect to read about in a feature article.

Next, present a model article and ask students to read the article while thinking about what makes the genre unique. You can choose to do this inquiry activity in whole group format reading aloud the article, or you can ask students to read the article silently. Remember to remind them that the purpose for reading is to identify elements of the genre. Following is a model feature article written in the Modern Language Association Research Style (Gibaldi, 2003), which is consistent with school-based research papers.

Model Feature Article: Women of the Mayflower: Weak or Willful?

Imagine spending 66 days on a 90-foot wooden ship with 101 other passengers and a crew of 30. As the ship crawls across the Atlantic at an average speed of under 2 miles per hour, strong storms and heavy crosswinds rock it, leaving the ship and its passengers weak. Leaking water drips between the floorboards and soaks the miserable seasick passengers living between the decks. Finally, after being thrown off-course and traveling 2750 miles, land is sighted. An anchor is dropped off the coast of Cape Cod and plans are made to come ashore. The men will gather firewood and explore this new world, while the 18 women onboard will go ashore ... to do the laundry!

The Pilgrims knew that the journey across the Atlantic would be long and dangerous, and that they would face even greater hardships when establishing the new colony. Governor William Bradford stated that the men feared the "weak bodies of the women and girls" would not be able to withstand these hardships, and Pilgrim husbands and fathers faced the difficult decision of whether to take their wives and daughters on the voyage or send for them later ("Girls on the Mayflower" 1).

Eighteen women, three of whom were pregnant, and eleven girls made the trip to America, which proved to be as difficult as anticipated. While no women or girls died on the trip itself, the first winter was brutal. The women and girls remained on board the Mayflower for four more months, while the men explored the area and built homes and storehouses. The damp and cramped quarters of the ship became a breeding ground for disease, and only five women survived the first winter. The girls fared better, and actually had a better survival rate than the men and boys. Only two girls died, while 50% of the men and 36% of the boys lost their lives ("Girls on the Mayflower" 1).

Although the survival rate was grim that first winter, the remaining women and older girls proved to be invaluable to the colonists. They cooked, cleaned, and did laundry for the entire colony. They also faced the task of raising the children who were orphaned during this time. While women were expected to be submissive and obey their husbands, the women of Plymouth gained some rights in the new land. They were allowed to buy, sell, and own property, and were given at least 1/3 of their husband's estate, even if the husband did not provide for it in his will. Women were allowed to be a legal witness for a deed or probate document, and they were also given more choice in deciding whom they would marry ("Women on the Mayflower" 1).

Where would America be today without these strong-willed women who first settled here? They not only raised their families in the new world, but also helped build the foundation that enabled later colonists to settle more easily. Today, there are a number of famous people who can trace their roots back to these first Pilgrims. Eight United States' presidents, including George W. Bush, actors such as Clint Eastwood, Marilyn Monroe, and Richard Gere, and the first American in space, Alan Shepard Jr., are all descendants of the Mayflower Pilgrims. This humble group of females, whose first chore in America was to do laundry, provided the quiet strength that allowed this nation to survive and grow to greatness ("Mayflower History" 1).

WORKS CITED

Johnson, C. *Girls on the* Mayflower. 2000. Mayflower Web Pages. 2 Feb. 2005. Available at: http://members.aol.com/calebj/girls.html

Johnson, C. *Women on the* Mayflower. 1998. Mayflower Web Pages. 2 Feb. 2005. Available at: http://members.aol.com/calebj/women.html

Johnson, C. Home page. 2005. MayflowerHistory.com. 2 Feb. 2005. Available at: http://www.mayflowerhistory.com/index.php

Elements of the Genre

Many of the elements of a feature newspaper article are similar to those found in any good piece of writing, yet there are some unique elements as well. As you guide students through this exercise of determining the genre elements, refer to Figure 4.1 for a description of elements commonly found in feature articles. Once students understand the type of writing they will be attempting, you can move onto the first planning step: topic selection. (Note: Appendix B contains full-size figures you can reproduce to make handouts and transparencies for your class.)

PLANNING STEP 1: SELECTING A TOPIC FOR THE FEATURE NEWSPAPER ARTICLE

The first step in writing a feature newspaper article is to help students select an interesting topic. If using a textbook in the content area, it may be helpful to discuss and record possible topics on chart paper and post it in the classroom as a unit is studied. Trade books can often provide glimpses of perspective, and may give students ideas for an angle to pursue further. Students must have a working knowledge of their topic and find it

Elements of a Feature Newspaper Article	
Lead	This introduces the topic and entices the reader through vivid word choice. A lead can start in a number of ways, such as a question, a quote, a startling fact, an anecdote, or a description that sets a scene.
Angle	This is the point of view or perspective from which the topic is explained. Writers must choose the focus of their articles and convey their views to others.
Factual Information	Regardless of the topic, factual information must support the writer's views and ideas. The writer may use examples, stories, quotes from experts or even everyday people, interviews, or statistics.
Organizational Structure	The writer must choose a text structure to present information, such as compare/contrast, cause/effect, sequential, problem/solution, different perspectives, or the pros and cons of an issue.
Author's Craft	Word choice, print features, and text features, such as charts, graphs, lists, maps, bulleted information, pictures, and time lines, all serve to clarify ideas.
Closure	The closing wraps up the writer's final thoughts about the topic.

Figure 4.1.   Elements of a feature newspaper article.

interesting, otherwise they will not be willing to invest the time needed to develop their pieces.

Initial Topic Selection

Once students are ready to select a topic, you should model the process for them. On an overhead projector, write a list of three to five possible topics and talk about each one, using a think aloud to share your thoughts with them. Next, select one topic to develop into a feature article and circle your choice, making sure to explain to students why that particular topic was chosen. At this point, in a guided practice format, students should follow the same process. In a "Writer's Notebook" or other similar recording folder, have your students generate a list of ideas they find interesting, and then give them time to share their ideas with a partner or small group to decide on the topic they would like to develop. The students can then circle the topic they have selected.

Expanding Topics

Next, ask students to think about what they already know and what questions they may have about their topic. As shown in Figure 4.2, you can draw a T-chart under your list, labeling one side "I Know..." and the other side "I Wonder..." and have the students do the same. This will help your students access background information and begin to organize their thoughts. Again, you should model your own ideas and questions culminating the activity by having the students complete their own T-charts.

To extend this activity, you can also begin to brainstorm possible resources needed to complete the research for a feature article. Under the T-chart, you can write the words "Possible Resources." Again using a think-aloud, model for students the types of sources you would consult to answer your questions. For example, some common information is best found in an encyclopedia, while some specific information may best be found in a primary source. Ask students to think about their information as they brainstorm resources they would consult. As students record their resources, you can offer suggestions as needed.

During this entire topic selection and brainstorm session, you may find that students do not have enough background knowledge about their topics so you may have to suggest that students conduct some preliminary research. In addition, students may need assistance to narrow their topics or suggestions to help clarify their thinking. The topics students choose should be challenging, but not to the point of frustration. If a student seems overwhelmed, he or she may need to select another topic from his preliminary list. Check in with each student to make sure his or her topic is appropriate.

Planning Step 2: Selecting an Audience and Purpose for Writing

Once students have selected their topics, they must think about their purpose for writing as well as the audience for whom they are writing. As suggested in Chapter 1, it is essential that students identify their purpose and audience early in the writing process because it helps focus their writing and influences their word choice. Figure 4.3 is a purpose and audience selection chart that you can use as you model this important step in the planning process.

Determining a Purpose for Writing

To determine the purpose for writing, ask students to consider how they want their readers to benefit from reading their article. Is it their intent to

Topic Selection for a Feature Newspaper Article

List some topics you are interested in and have some knowledge about:

1. _____

2. _____

3. _____

4. _____

5. _____

I know...   *I wonder...*

Possible resources:

_____

_____

_____

_____

_____

_____

_____

Figure 4.2.   Choosing a topic for a feature newspaper article.

**How to Choose a Purpose and Audience
for a Feature Newspaper Article**

My topic is: _____

First, ask yourself, what is my purpose for writing?

- To notify?
- To amuse?
- To share?
- To convince?
- Other?

Therefore, my purpose for writing is:

_____

_____

_____

Next, consider your audience.

Am I writing for:

- Someone who knows very little about my topic? ___
- Someone who is an expert on my topic? ___
- Someone who is much younger than I? ___

Therefore, my audience is:

_____

_____

_____

Figure 4.3.   Purpose and audience selection for a feature newspaper article.

notify? To amuse? To share? To convince? Model for students how to think about these questions to determine the purpose of a feature article. Then ask students to consider those essential questions to determine their purpose and record it in their Writer's Notebook or on a sheet of paper.

Selecting an Audience

Equally as important is to have students think about their audience. Who might be interested in reading about their topic? Why? Is their audience made up of experts on the topic or novices? Will they need to explain in detail? You should model audience selection and instruct students to do the same.

Have students use their purpose and audience statements as a point of reference throughout the composition process. Remember to use the information in Chapter 1 in regard to the relationship between purpose, audience and word choice to help students refine their feature articles. If students remain consistent with their purpose and audience, their writing will be focused and word choice will be considerate to their readers.

PLANNING STEP 3: RESEARCHING, RECORDING AND ORGANIZING INFORMATION

Now that students have identified their topic, purpose, and audience, they will need to begin their research. The questions they generated on their T-chart should be used as a starting point and students can begin to select their first sources. Keeping information and thoughts organized during this process is crucial! If students are not using a Writer's Notebook, the teacher should provide them with a folder to keep materials in one place.

Your school librarian can help you and your students select appropriate sources for their newspaper projects. Also note that there should be clear criteria about the sources, such as a minimum number or the types of sources that can be used. Explicit modeling of note-taking strategies such as using keywords or paraphrasing to gather information without plagiarizing sources will help facilitate this process if students are not familiar with research strategies. A graphic organizer such as the one found in Figure 4.4 can assist the note-taking process. I found that using a chart format is easier for note taking than small index cards that get lost in backpacks. Because space is limited, students cannot copy large amounts of information and must paraphrase or use keywords. Students also start to synthesize their information from multiple sources, which may help determine their angle. At this point, you may wish to model a standard note-taking process.

To help students with information needs, you may need to point out interesting statistics, pictures, or other text features that may be used when writing the feature article. It is helpful to record these sources so they can be accessed easily later on, as well as used when students cite their sources.

PLANNING STEP 4: SELECTING AN ANGLE

During the research process, the students' initial topics should begin to grow and become more refined. As students look at their findings and start drawing conclusions about information, they may discover the angle that

Note-sheet Graphic Organizer for Researching Feature Article Stories			
	Source 1 Title/Web site:	Source 2 Title/Web site:	Source 3 Title/Web site:
Idea/Question			
Idea/Question			
Idea/Question			

Figure 4.4.   Note-sheet graphic organizer for researching feature article stories.

they will use to present their information. Sometimes common threads develop among the sources checked, or perhaps the student has a question that leads them to an interesting perspective to pursue. Once students have a fair amount of information, you should model choosing an angle for your topic or for one a student has chosen. You can do this by using the model essay presented earlier in this chapter. Discuss how the author of this piece chose to take the angle of the Pilgrim women's strength and vitality beginning with the question posed in the title: *Women of the Mayflower: Weak or Willful?* and following through to the end positing that the Pilgrim women were willful and strong. You can discuss the various angles you may have used to present your topic. For example, you may have focused on the bravery of one specific woman colonist or you may have chosen to focus on the courage of the male colonists. Have students try out selecting their angles and conclude this planning step by conferring with each student and assisting as needed.

PLANNING STEP 5: SELECTING AN ORGANIZING STRUCTURE

Just as the angle frequently unfolds during the research process, so does the organizing structure that can be used to present students' information. For example, some topics are clearly chronological, causal, or problem/solution; others may involve pros and cons or perhaps present different perspectives of a topic. At this point, you may wish to model the process of choosing an organizing structure for a topic. Try using the think-aloud method to show the options considered and then decide on an organizing structure.

Students need time to select their organizing structure, which may be done independently, with a peer, or with you. You can then provide students with an appropriate graphic organizer to assist them in writing their rough draft. A sample model for a pro/con text structure has been provided for you in Figure 4.5. At this stage, some students may find they have all the information they need, while others may need further research to fill in some gaps.

PLANNING STEP 6: WRITING A LEAD

There are a number of ways to start a feature article, and reading some good examples is a great way to motivate students. Present your students with clear examples that you extract from the daily newspaper. Demonstrate starting the article with an anecdote or an interesting quote, and discuss whether that particular lead was effective for the article.

Students must understand the power of a good lead explained in the following items:

1. It must be appealing and attract their readers to read on.

2. It must suggest their topic.

3. It must provide a smooth transition to the information following.

Next, model writing the lead, showing at least two different options and discussing which one works better. Then, have students compose leads for their topic trying out various types. Students can then share their leads with a partner and discuss the one they feel is most effective.

Graphic Organizer for the Feature Article Rough Draft

Introduction or short anecdote providing background information:

_____

_____

_____

_____

Body: Choose graphic organizer to suit text structure.
            (Sample below includes one for the pros and cons of an issue.)

Pros	*Cons*

Concluding main points:

_____

_____

_____

_____

Figure 4.5.   Graphic organizer for feature newspaper article.

COMPOSING THE ROUGH DRAFT

Students' ideas should be well organized by this point, and they should be ready to compose their rough drafts. Now it is time to bring everything together.

As with the previous steps, model a portion of writing your rough draft. Start with the lead selected earlier and demonstrate the transition to the body of the article. When writing the body, show students how to follow the organizing text structure chosen earlier and also discuss the text features that are most effective in communicating ideas. Should facts or statistics be listed in a fact box, bulleted, or incorporated within the paragraph? Would a timeline be helpful in showing a sequence of events? Would pictures or a diagram help clarify the topic? There are numerous techniques that can be used, and students need to see them demonstrated to get ideas for their own writing. Students should write their rough drafts, keeping in mind that this is a first attempt to get their thoughts on paper and they will revise later.

Closure

The final piece of the feature article is the closing. This is just as important as the lead, because it wraps up ideas and hopefully leaves a lingering impression on the reader. Again, you will need to model this step to demonstrate how important ideas are tied together and brought to a significant closure. You can use newspaper articles to show how writers close their pieces so there is no question in the reader's mind how the writer feels about the topic.

REVISING AND EDITING THE ROUGH DRAFT

All too often students want to omit the revision and editing processes, feeling their rough draft is perfect as is or that they only need to look for misspelled words. Students need to understand the difference between the two steps and showing, rather than telling, is key.

To help with this process, try putting your own or a student's rough draft on the overhead. Then read it out loud to the students, explaining that you want to make sure the writing (a) is clear to the reader, (b) presents organized ideas, and (c) contains word choice that conveys the information in an accurate and interesting way.

After the initial reading, you can demonstrate some revision strategies, including how to improve transitions, clarify wording, or perhaps change the text features originally chosen so the writing flows more easily or is more understandable to readers. Revision mini-lessons should help students with organization, word choice, sentence structure, and text features (Calkins, 1994).

They may also need guidance in strengthening their leads and closings and choosing a title. Focus on one revision strategy at a time and have students apply it to their writing after it is modeled. Students also need to consider the layout of their final drafts, such as placement of pictures, fact boxes, or timelines.

Finally, have students edit their piece for conventions. Choose mini-lessons that meet the needs of the students, modeling first in the context of a writing piece, and then have students check their writing (Weaver, 1996). Students should self-edit, then peer-edit, and confer with you for best overall results.

PUBLISHING AND SHARING THE FINAL DRAFT

After all their hard work, students are probably very anxious to complete their finished piece. Whether hand-written or word-processed, students need to be mindful as they are writing to make sure they include their revision and editing corrections. In addition to adding their pictures, charts, or diagrams, students may also use print features, such as bold or italicized print, to bring attention to certain points. Have students proofread their piece one last time to make sure they are satisfied with the finished product and that it meets the criteria of the assignment. Finally, give the students the opportunity to share their writing with others. After all, their purpose in writing is to communicate their findings to their audience!

EVALUATING THE FINAL DRAFT

The final piece that students submit for evaluation should represent their best work. As suggested in Chapter 1, provide students with the rubric you will use to evaluate their writing early in the drafting process and refer to it as you work through the drafting, revising, and editing stages. If students understand the evaluation criteria *before* they complete the drafts of their feature articles, they will work toward meeting the performance criteria included on the feature article rubric included in Appendix A. Finally, share the results of your evaluation with students to help them identify specific writing strengths and challenges. In order for our students to grow as writers, we must build on their strengths, provide feedback for improving weak areas, and continue to encourage them in their writing.

CHAPTER 5

THE NARRATIVE PROCEDURE

The "How-To" Essay

Katharine Laura Canole

THE NATURE OF THE GENRE

What is a narrative procedure? A narrative is a story told to someone else. A procedure is a particular way of doing something or a series of steps that should be followed in a specific, chronological order. Therefore, a narrative procedure is an explanation of how to do something. While writing a narrative procedure, your students will provide directions, or the necessary steps, that must be followed in order to achieve or complete a task (National Center on Education, 1997).

You may ask students to write a narrative procedure for a variety of different tasks or topics. Some examples of narrative procedures, as cited in the *New Standards Performance Standards* (1997), include (a) setting rules for organizing a class meeting, (b) instructions for playing a game, (c) instructions for using media technology, (d) an explanation of a mathematic procedure, (e) directions to a home, or (f) directions to make a family recipe. When one explains in prose how to do something step-by-step, the resulting essay is called a narrative procedure. You can see that a narrative procedure is an outstanding way to have your students implement writing across the curriculum.

Teaching Writing Genres Across the Curriculum, pages 63–76
Copyright © 2006 by Information Age Publishing
All rights of reproduction in any form reserved.

Clearly explaining to another person how to accomplish something is a skill that your students will appreciate in a variety of different situations. In this chapter, the steps that your students will follow to complete the process of writing a narrative procedure are presented in a clear and easy to follow manner.

INTRODUCING THE GENRE: USING A MODEL ESSAY TO EXEMPLIFY THE GENRE

In order to give students an idea of what the genre *looks like*, it is a good idea to have them read a model essay and think about what makes this genre different or similar to other writing genres. Following is a model narrative procedure essay. The topic of this model is *How to Write a Narrative Procedure*. Before students read it silently, point out how the model explains the step-by-step process of writing a narrative procedure. Also ask them to pay attention to what elements make up the genre. Your goal is to have students understand the *nature of the genre*. Following is a model essay you can use to accomplish this goal.

Model Essay: How to Write a Narrative Procedure
   Writing a narrative procedure is easy if you know the correct steps. I bet you know much more about this type of writing than you think you do, but I'd like to give you a few hints to remind you of things you may have forgotten. To write a narrative procedure, you will need three things: paper, pen (or pencil), and a fairly extensive amount of knowledge of your topic.
   The first step to writing such a piece of work is choosing your topic. Once you have a topic you must choose your audience and set your purpose. The next step can be fairly extensive; you must brainstorm about your selected topic. Be sure to record all of your ideas so that you can decide whether or not you know enough about the topic to explain it to someone else. Once you have your ideas on paper you must organize them using a graphic organizer. When your organization is complete the hard part is over.
   Now it is time to begin your first draft. If you have clear and detailed notes, this should be fairly easy. An important part of drafting is developing a "lead" or an interesting first line. If you don't catch your reader's attention right away, he or she may choose to look through the bookshelves for something better to read. After your lead is developed you will write an introduction to launch your reader into the purpose of your paper.

After completing your introduction you are ready to begin listing your steps, or drafting your steps in paragraph form. Be sure to write your steps in the correct order so your reader does not get confused. Between each step you must include a transition word, or phrase, to bridge, or connect your steps together, making them easier to follow. After including all of the necessary steps, check to make sure that you have been clear and to the point. Check to see if you are missing any information that is necessary to the reader. For example, you must include definitions for unfamiliar terms, or examples to clarify your topic. You may even choose to add a glossary at the end of your essay if there are several unfamiliar terms. Sometimes it is helpful to include a picture, graphic, map, or reference to assist your reader in his or her understanding. Once you have completed your draft, read your essay aloud to make sure that it makes sense to you.

Now comes the fun part: peer revision. Trade papers with a partner and read them aloud. Discuss your papers using constructive criticism. Do not write on your partner's paper; that is his job, but be sure to give your opinions about his paper. You may recommend some things to help your partner improve his paper or you may ask questions for further clarification. Note the purpose, audience, and some specific words that help illustrate the purpose and audience of your partner's paper.

When you get your own paper back, revise any sections that remain confusing. You may cross out, add additional lines, or change whole paragraphs. Don't leave writing that is not your best.

Finally, look for any areas that need editing. Fix any spelling, grammar, or sentence structure errors; you may work with your partner for this as well. Once you are confident with your paper, you can write or type a final draft. If you follow these easy steps, soon the process of writing a narrative procedure will become second nature and you will no longer need your teacher's help.

Elements of the Genre

As described in Chapter 1, this step of the process is essential to having students understand the nature of the genre. Once students have read the model essay, have them try to brainstorm what makes this genre unique. To help with your lesson, a list of elements commonly found in the narrative procedure genre is included in Figure 5.1. (Note: Appendix B contains full-size figures you can reproduce to make handouts and transparencies for your class.)

Elements of a Narrative Procedure

1. *A good narrative procedure is well organized.* The paper includes a clear introduction, body, and conclusion. In addition, there are clear transitions between each section.

2. *A good narrative procedure has a clear purpose.* The paper begins by stating the task being explained so the reader immediately understands the purpose of your paper.

3. *A good narrative procedure has logical steps.* The steps of the procedure are clear and easy to follow. They are based on fact, expert opinions, and/or personal experiences.

4. *A good narrative procedure has a clearly defined audience.* The audience, or for whom the writer is writing, should be clear and consistent throughout the paper. Writers must choose if they are writing for someone who has no experience with the procedure, some experience, or much experience. Writers must choose just one audience, the novice or the expert, and be consistent throughout the paper.

5. *A good narrative procedure has correct use of English language conventions.* The writer demonstrates an understanding of all rules of the English language.

Figure 5.1.   Elements of a narrative procedure.

PLANNING STEP 1: SELECTING A TOPIC FOR THE NARRATIVE PROCEDURE

The first step in *preparing* to write a narrative procedure is to determine the topic and brainstorm personal knowledge of the topic. To write an explanation or a set of directions, your students will need to have enough familiarity with the chosen task that they will be able to provide clear and easy-to-follow instructions. Be sure to remind them of this during topic selection. Topic selection is broken down into several sections for better understanding and clarification of the teaching process.

Teaching Students to Select an Initial Topic

When writing a narrative procedure your students are teaching someone else how to do something so they need to have a clear understanding of the topic themselves. In other words, they must have some prior experience with this topic. To assist you in teaching topic selection, model for students how to ask themselves the following questions:

- What is it that you want to write about?
- What procedure do you find interesting and think others would enjoy learning?

- With what type of procedure are you very familiar?
- What do you know how to do very well and could easily teach someone else?

Once you have brainstormed several possible topics, have students brainstorm their own topics. You may, of course, choose to give students an initial topic frame. For example, you can ask students to write a procedure for any mathematical operation or science experiment they learned during your course of study. Once students have an initial topic, you want to be sure it is not too broad to compose a specific narrative procedure. Following is a teaching step for narrowing topic choices.

Teaching Students to Narrow an Initial Topic

Ask your students to look at your list of possible initial topics they generated earlier and select one in which they have the most knowledge. Ask them to write down the topic and then list or web their knowledge and experience with it. If your students realize that they do not have a good deal of knowledge or experience with their topics, encourage them to choose another topic and begin the narrowing process again. Figure 5.2 is a graphic organizer designed to help students with this step.

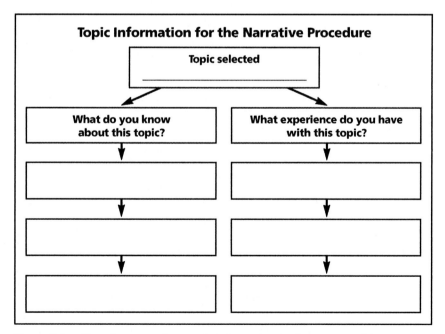

Figure 5.2. Narrative procedure topic information brainstorm graphic.

Students Share Their Topics

In order for students to have a true concept of audience and gather feedback about their topics, it is a good idea to have students share their topics and their knowledge and experiences about their topics with a partner. You can model for your students how to do this by choosing one student to share his/her responses with you in front of the whole class. The following questions can be used to guide your modeling:

- Does this sound like an interesting topic?
- Is it something you might want to learn about?
- Does it sound like I have enough prior knowledge and experience to do a good job explaining this topic to my reader?
- If I don't have enough information or experience, is it something that I can easily find out?
- Will this topic be too complicated to explain?

Once you have modeled this process, ask students to work in pairs to share their topics. When they have completed this task, ask the students to review their graphic organizers and ask themselves the following questions:

- Can I add any more information?
- Do I need to do some research to expand my knowledge before I begin writing?

Planning Step 2: Selecting an Audience and Purpose for Writing

All good writing has one common feature: a specific audience. It is necessary for writers to be aware of and considerate to their readers throughout their work. The words and the explanations students provide should be the direct result of their choice of audience.

This is especially important when writing a narrative procedure. Students need to keep in mind that the purpose of this style of writing is to teach someone else how something works, how to get somewhere, or how to do or make something, thus the audience needs to understand each and every step. To have students give careful consideration to a chosen audience, you will need to model for them how you choose an audience. Figure 5.3 has a list of questions designed to assist students to pinpoint their exact audience.

After students have determined their audience, it is a good idea to have them work with varying purposes. A narrative procedure is informational and can be on any topic in many different situations. To help your students

---

Determine Your Audience for the Narrative Procedure

1. **For whom** am I writing?

2. **What age are my readers?**
   Are they older, younger, or the same age as I am? The answers to these questions will help you decide the type of words to use. The vocabulary you choose will reflect the skill level of the reader.

3. **Are my readers beginners or experienced with this topic?**
   These answers will help you to determine how much, or how little detail you need in your writing. If a reader is a beginner, you will need to include much background knowledge. If your reader is experienced you will need less background knowledge, appealing to his or her expertise.

4. **What will be the most complex piece of the topic for my reader?**
   This answer will help you to establish the areas that you will need to provide more details and examples to assist your readers.

Figure 5.3.   Audience selection for a narrative procedure.

define a clear purpose for writing you must first model for them how to determine a clear purpose by using the following questions:

- Why am I writing this piece?
- What is my goal for my reader? To learn the procedure? To have them become familiar with the procedure?
- What word choice is appropriate for my chosen audience?

This planning will help students accomplish the simple formula discussed in Chapter 1: *Purpose +Audience= Word Choice*. If you have already presented the lesson from Chapter 1, you can extend the thinking to this narrative procedure by placing on a transparency the following chart and asking students to think about the purpose, audience and word choice appropriate for this genre and their chosen topics. The first one is completed for you illustrating the change in word choice as a result in audience change.

Type	Purpose	Audience	Word Choice
A complicated family recipe	*To teach*	People who enjoy cooking and entertaining	"A bit complicated" "Light and fluffy" "Delicious" "Takes time to learn the process"
		— versus —	
		Experienced chefs	"Easy for the experienced" "No time at all" "Light and fluffy" "Delicious"
Directions from one place on a map to another			
Instructions for writing a math proof			

PLANNING STEP 3: BRAINSTORMING, RECORDING, AND ORGANIZING INFORMATION

Brainstorming and recording information is the most complex step in the narrative procedure writing process. During this step, students must plan all of their ideas and see what works, what doesn't work, what is missing, and what should be cut. Once they have listed all of their steps, they will have the bulk of the information that will make up their first drafts. For your ease of teaching this step, the process is explained in short lessons.

Writing the Thesis Statement

To help students frame their pieces, have them begin by creating a thesis statement. If students are unfamiliar with writing thesis statements, explain that the thesis informs the reader of the main idea and goal of the piece of writing. This is a time when they need to incorporate their purpose, audience, and topic. To help write the thesis statement, have the students ask themselves the following questions:

- What is my purpose?
- What do I want my readers to learn from reading my piece?

Next, your students need to be directed while writing a statement that lets their readers know exactly what the paper is about. The thesis statement should be a declarative sentence that is clear, direct, and explicit. For example, have them consider the thesis statement for the model essay included in this chapter:

To write a narrative procedure, you will need three things: paper, pen (or pencil), and a fairly extensive amount of knowledge of your topic.

Once you have described thesis statements and provided students with a few examples, ask students to compose their own thesis statements and share them in small groups asking peers to help with revision suggestions.

Listing the Materials Needed for "How-to" Narrative Procedures

One piece of brainstorming that is unique to narrative procedure writing is a list of the materials needed for "how-to" types of writing. For example, if your students are explaining how to make a necklace, they must inform the reader of everything they must have in order to create the piece of jewelry. This includes the pieces that go into the actual necklace as well as the tools needed to manipulate the pieces. It is also helpful to give an estimated amount of time the project or procedure will take. Have students make a simple list so they will be sure to include them in the appropriate section of their narratives. For example:

Materials:
Tools:
Time Needed:

Organizing the Information To Prepare for Drafting

The final step in the planning process is *essential.* You may feel compelled to skip this step and have students begin drafting; however, I have found that it is very important for students to outline and organize their steps and facts *before* they begin drafting for a better outcome. To complete this important planning step, you can have students organize their steps and details into a sequential graphic organizer. For this teaching step, you will have to model for your students how to refine the information and record it into a graphic organizer. I have used the simple graphic displayed in Figure 5.4 with exceptional success.

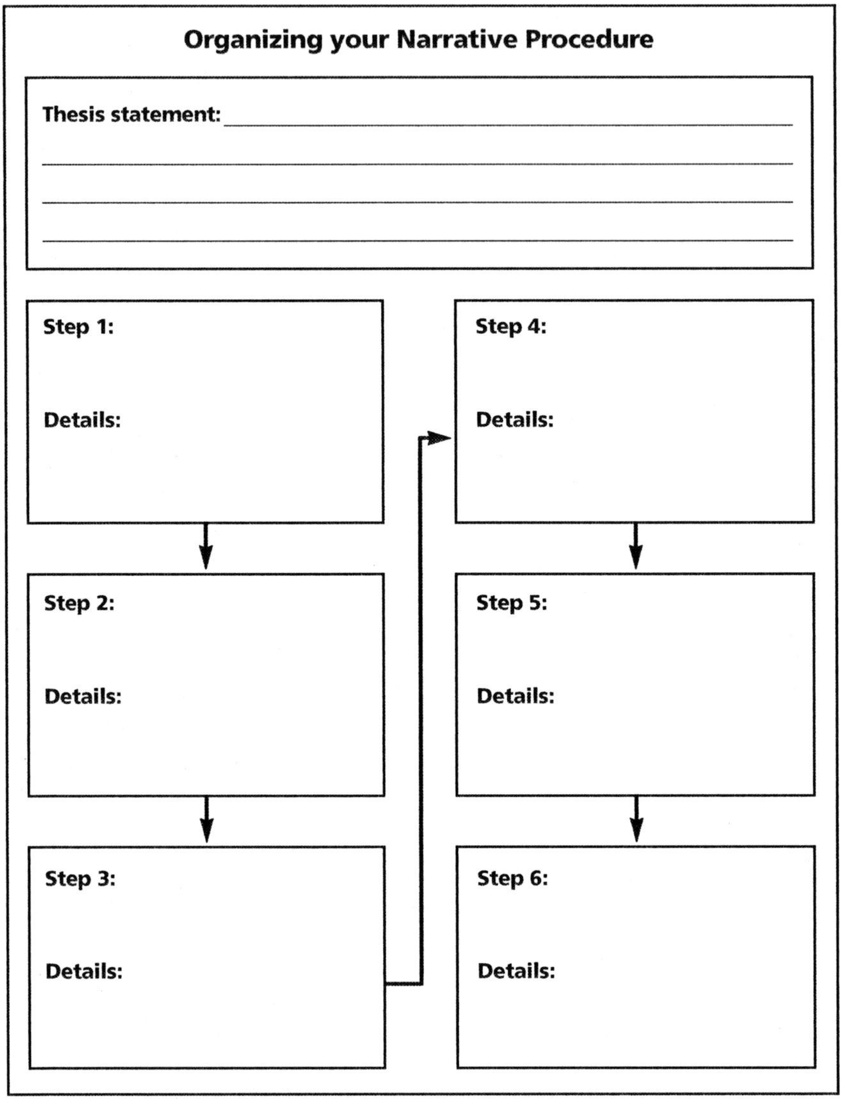

Organizing your Narrative Procedure

Thesis statement: _____
_____
_____
_____

Step 1:

Details:

Step 4:

Details:

Step 2:

Details:

Step 5:

Details:

Step 3:

Details:

Step 6:

Details:

Figure 5.4.   Narrative procedure final planning organizer.

Following is a partially completed organizer based on the model essay provided in this chapter. You can use this to model how to complete the organizer for your students or use one of your students' topics to model this process.

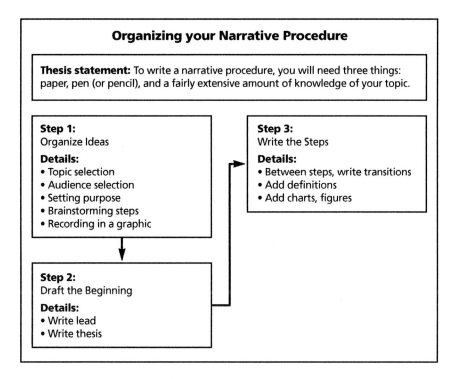

Organizing your Narrative Procedure

Thesis statement: To write a narrative procedure, you will need three things: paper, pen (or pencil), and a fairly extensive amount of knowledge of your topic.

Step 1:
Organize Ideas

Details:
• Topic selection
• Audience selection
• Setting purpose
• Brainstorming steps
• Recording in a graphic

Step 3:
Write the Steps

Details:
• Between steps, write transitions
• Add definitions
• Add charts, figures

Step 2:
Draft the Beginning

Details:
• Write lead
• Write thesis

As you model, remind students that it is important to list the steps in the order in which they occur. Also explain that this step is important because it adds clarity to the narrative procedure and assures that students think about the order of the procedure as well as the details that correspond with each step. Once students have completed their own graphic organizers, they then can use them as an outline for their rough drafts.

COMPOSING THE ROUGH DRAFT

Once students have completed their graphic organizers, their thoughts are now organized and the narrative procedure steps are in the appropriate order. This will make writing the first draft a fairly smooth process. However, there are still several steps that must be taken while drafting. Writing a narrative procedure is just like writing any other expository genre: there must be an introductory paragraph, body paragraphs, and a conclusion paragraph.

Modeling How to Compose the Introduction

The introduction consists of three specific pieces: the lead, the main points of the paper, and the thesis statement. Model for students how to do the following:

1. Begin with the lead, which is an interesting statement, anecdote, or quotation that will catch the reader's attention and hold it.
2. Write the main points that will be covered in the body of the narrative procedure.
3. Include a thesis statement at the beginning, middle, or end of the introductory paragraph.

Modeling How to Compose the Body

The body of your students' papers will consist primarily of the steps involved in the narrative procedure. Remind students that their writing should always be in their own words unless they are using a direct quotation from their research sources. Following are other considerations while drafting that you might want students to think about:

1. Consider their audience as they write, always choosing appropriate words and phrases for that audience. For example, if they are writing for an audience that has no prior knowledge of the topic, they need to use clear, simple language being very careful to define ideas and terms that are complex or may be unfamiliar.
2. Write interesting topic sentences that clue readers into what will be in each paragraph.
3. Include important, relevant details that support their topic sentences.
4. Use transition words and phrases to improve the flow of their writing and to keep the reader on track. This is particularly important in narrative procedure writing because they are explaining many steps to the reader.

Modeling How to Compose the Conclusion

The conclusion consists of three specific pieces that fit together in a particular order: the summary, the reiteration of the thesis statement, and the closing statement. Remind students to do the following:

1. Begin with the summary; recap the main points of the paper.

2. Rework the thesis statement. It should be reiterated, not restated.
3. End with a strong closing statement that leaves a lasting impression on the reader.

REVISING AND EDITING THE ROUGH DRAFT

As you already know, the rough draft is far from a finished product; it is just the beginning. Explain to your students that once they have a completed draft, they are ready to revise the ideas, word choice, and sentence or paragraph structure. Following are the important instructional guidelines to remind your students about the revision and editing processes.

1. The *act of revision* is to improve the piece. During revision, students work on the presentation of ideas, organizational structure, sentence structure, paragraph structure, and word choice (Graves, 1983).
2. The *act of editing* is purely mechanical. This is the final combing of the paper for grammar and mechanics errors such as grammar, punctuation, capitalization, and spelling (Calkins, 1994, Graves, 1983).
3. Students should *set their drafts aside* for at least 24 hours to gain some distance from the piece. After that they should have one or more peers discuss and help revise and edit their drafts. After conferring, students should make more revision and editing changes.
4. Remind students that good writers *accomplish multiple drafts* before being satisfied with their work.

PUBLISHING AND SHARING THE FINAL DRAFT

You and your students have made it to the final step! During this last stage of the process, students should clean up their final drafts; add any illustrations, diagrams, tables, or charts that may help them to make the narrative procedure even better than it already is, as well as helping the reader visualize the steps. Following are final strategies for helping your students complete their final drafts:

1. Have them *make a title page.*
2. *Review their final drafts* to be sure that all of the pages are included and in the proper order.
3. *Share* their papers with class, family, and friends to drive home the concept of audience.

EVALUATING THE FINAL DRAFT

I have included an analytic evaluation rubric in Appendix A. This type of rubric is used so students can see the various things they did well in addition to the writing components that need to be improved.

The rubric is designed to assess the five elements of narrative procedure writing. These elements have been the focus for the entire unit so the students are being assessed on what they have been explicitly taught. I always distribute and review the rubric at the start of the unit so students understand exactly what I expect from them. As presented in Chapter 1, if students understand the evaluation criteria before they finish their narrative procedures, they will work toward meeting the highest performance expectations. It also takes the mystery out of grading. Students are aware from the start what I expect and what they must do to earn a quality grade; thus frustrations and arguments about grades are avoided.

CHAPTER 6

WRITTEN RESPONSE TO MATHEMATICAL QUESTIONS

Computation and Composition

Suzanne Madden Scallin

THE NATURE OF THE GENRE

Open-response questions are an integral component of a mathematics curriculum (National Council of Teachers of Mathematics, 2000). An open-response question requires the students to combine mathematics knowledge with their writing skills in order to effectively communicate both their answer and the process used to solve the problem. An open response question may have one correct answer or there may be multiple answers. In addition, an open response question often has more than one possible way to solve it. Responding to open-response questions helps students to better understand mathematical concepts and the processes they are using to solve problems (National Council of Teachers of Mathematics, 2000). Incorporating process into our mathematical thinking will help our students internalize the knowledge and be able to apply the knowledge in real life.

Teaching Writing Genres Across the Curriculum, pages 77–90
Copyright © 2006 by Information Age Publishing
77

Teachers, responding to national standards, find that they must now teach writing in addition to grade level math content. In many districts, mathematics teachers struggle with teaching students writing since they have had no preparation for doing so. This chapter is a summary of my attempt to teach students the practice of writing open responses. I hope it will help you break down the teaching of this fundamental skill.

INTRODUCING THE GENRE: USING A MODEL RESPONSE TO EXEMPLIFY THE GENRE

Model Response

The first step in teaching students how to write a response to open-ended questions is to introduce students to the genre by presenting them with a model response. The purpose of this exercise is to have students think about what is included in a response. It also helps to introduce them to (a) the word choice and math vocabulary used in a response, (b) the format appropriate to a response, and (c) what a completed response looks like. I have included an example of a question and response as part of this text to use as a model for your students. After you look over the model, I give suggestions for how to introduce it to your students.

Question. A group of students recorded the attendance data for their homeroom over two weeks. The results are shown in this table:

Homeroom Attendance Data	
Date	Students Present (Total 21 students)
December 5	19
December 6	21
December 7	20
December 8	19
December 9	18
December 12	17
December 13	19
December 14	15
December 15	16
December 16	20

1. Create a table using the information above that will show the attendance data as a fraction and as a percent.
2. Create a stem and leaf plot of the attendance data using the percentages.
3. What is the mode of the attendance data?
4. What is the mean of the attendance data?
5. What is the median of the attendance data? Show or explain your work.

Response.

A. Table of Attendance Data as Fraction and Percent

Date	Students Present (Total 21 students)	Fraction of students present	Percent of students present
December 5	19	19/21	90%
December 6	21	21/21	100%
December 7	20	20/21	95%
December 8	19	19/21	90%
December 9	18	18/21	86%
December 12	17	17/21	81%
December 13	19	19/21	90%
December 14	15	15/21	71%
December 15	16	16/21	76%
December 16	20	20/21	95%

The table above shows the attendance data as fractions and as percents. I found the fraction by recording the number of students present over the total number of students. The number of students present is the numerator because it is the number of parts of the whole that are being considered. The total number of students is the denominator because it is the number of parts that make up the whole. I found the percent of students present by dividing the numerator by the denominator and changing the quotient to a decimal. My quotients were decimals. I know that .90 is read ninety hundredths, which is equal to 90%.

Example
$19 \div 21 = .904761$, which when rounded to the nearest tenth is .90
$.90 = 90/100 = 90\%$

B. Gathering the data for the stem and leaf plot

90	71
100	76
95	81
90	86
86	90
81	90
90	91
71	95
76	95
95	100

Homeroom Attendance Percentages

Stem	Leaf
7	16
8	16
9	00155
10	0

Key 6|8 = 68

I created a stem and leaf plot of the attendance percentages. To do this I first listed the data from least to greatest. Next, I used the numbers in the tens or hundreds place as my stem and the numbers in the ones place as my leaves.

C.The mode of the students present is 90%. Mode is the value that appears most often in the data. 90% appears three times.

D.The mean of the attendance data is 87%. Mean is the average of a set of numbers. To find the mean I found the sum of the attendance percentages and divided by the number of percents.

90	
100	$874 \div 10 = 87.4$
95	
90	87.4 rounded to nearest whole number is 87
86	
81	
90	
71	
76	
+ 95	
874	

E. The median of the attendance data is 90%. The median is the middle value in a list of statistics ordered from least to greatest. To find this I listed the data from least to greatest and found that 90 is the percentage in the middle.

Data	Data from least to greatest
90	71
100	76
95	81
90	86
86	90
81	90
90	91
71	95
76	95
95	100

Elements of the Genre

As described in Chapter 1, identifying the elements of the genre is important for students to truly see what a good open response contains. Once students have read the model essay, invite them to brainstorm the elements that make this genre unique. To guide you through this lesson, a list of elements commonly found in the math open response is included in Figure 6.1. (Note: Appendix B contains full-size figures you can reproduce to make handouts and transparencies for your class.)

Elements of a Math Response

- Writing should include responses to all parts of the question.
- There should be connections between each step.
- Each part of the question should be labeled.
- Organization should match the sequential nature of answering the question.
- The sequence of steps to solve and the strategy used should be included.
- The writing explains to the reader each step of the process needed to solve the problem.
- Mathematics content specific vocabulary is used throughout the response.
- The writing includes graphs, charts, number lines and diagrams as needed.
- Definitions for vocabulary words are included to demonstrate understanding.
- There needs to be evidence of computation with correct results.
- Editing is important! The writing demonstrates an understanding of spelling, grammar, and mechanics.

Figure 6.1.   Elements of a mathematical response to an open ended question.

As students "debrief" the model,·have them identify and talk about the elements of the genre. Later, when students are drafting their own first responses, you can refer back to this model to have them "check" to see if they have all the elements included.

The following procedural steps were written with reference to many sources, including the Kentucky Department of Education, 1997, The National Council of Teachers of Mathematics Problem Solving Strategies, 2000, and Math Counts, 2003.

PLANNING STEP 1: SELECTING AN AUDIENCE AND PURPOSE FOR WRITING

The purpose of responding to an open response question in math is to demonstrate knowledge of mathematical content and process. The writer is explaining to the reader the solution to the problem and all the steps of the process necessary to complete the problem. Be sure that students know their purpose in writing a response is to answer the question and explain their processes.

In selecting an audience, the writer should consider the level of mathematical knowledge of the reader. Are they writing for their teachers? Their peers? If so, they may use word choice appropriate to the classroom instruction. If they are writing for a younger audience, they will have to be much more explicit and the writing will be more extensive.

To help students identify their audiences, refer to Figure 6.2. This audience selection will help you to guide students' thinking about audience and understand the importance of being explicit, clear, and direct in their responses.

Questions to Ask to Help Determine Your Math Response Audience

- Does the person reading this have the same degree of mathematical knowledge as I do? Do they have more or less?
- Do they share a common math vocabulary with me? Do I need to explain the meaning of vocabulary?
- Did this person already solve this problem? Is my purpose to show evidence that I can solve the problem?
- Is my audience my teacher, peers, younger children, or adults?
- Is my reader assessing my knowledge? or Am I simply explaining the process to my readers?

Figure 6.2.   Audience selection for the math response.

PLANNING STEP 3: BRAINSTORMING, RECORDING, AND ORGANIZING INFORMATION

The next step is the longest step. It requires the most time and modeling. Figure 6.3 is a flow chart that you can place on the overhead projector as you model each step. In addition, to guide your modeling, I have included a step-by-step lesson plan.

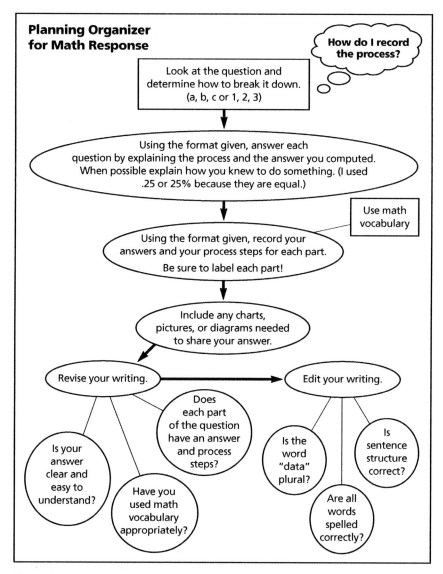

Figure 6.3.   Planning organizer for math response.

Modeling How to Identify the Question Parts

One of the problems I have encountered in teaching students to write a response occurs early on in the process. It is extremely important that students truly understand the question and its parts. Of course, it will be easier for students to understand the question parts if you design questions that have very specific parts and label them with an a, b, c, or a 1, 2, 3 format.

As you model for students how to attend to the initial question parts, I suggest that you model the following:

1. Carefully read the question aloud and locate all important information and data. Model for students how to locate the question parts and circle each one.
2. Next, as each part of the information needed is considered, have students identify the data to use for that part.

Modeling How to Answer Each Question Part

Another area in which students have difficulty is isolating the answer to each question part. You will notice that in my model response, I have carefully labeled and identified each answer. Show students how to label and identify each part.

Once students have an idea of how to approach answering each question part, you can model how to explicitly explain the process of computation. It is important to remind students that whenever possible, they should explain how they "knew" something. For example, in my model, I state:

"The median is the middle value in a list of statistics ordered from least to greatest. To find this I listed the data from least to greatest and found that 90 is the percentage in the middle."

(The second sentence above explains how I knew that the median is the middle value of statistics.)

Modeling How to Use Content Specific Vocabulary

As students begin to work on answering their questions, another lesson you may present at this time is using mathematical vocabulary in their responses. You can do this simply by using the model response and underlining the use of the mathematical vocabulary. For example:

The number of students present is the numerator because it is the number of parts of the whole that are being considered. The total number of students is the denominator because it is the number of parts that make up the whole.

The use of appropriate content specific vocabulary can make the difference between a mediocre response and a superior one. The students will begin to internalize this as they begin practicing. As students begin to produce responses, you may also choose to put an exemplary student model of explicit use of mathematical terms on the overhead projector. This instructional step will extend the modeling and coaching of this important element.

Modeling How to Use Diagrams, Charts, and Pictures

As students work through their responses, you may wish to provide lessons as needed to update students' skill in designing appropriate charts, diagrams, and pictures.

COMPOSING THE ROUGH DRAFT

Modeling the Opening

As students begin to acquire the information for their drafts, it is important to model how to begin the introduction to the response. The writer needs to remember that this form of writing is in response to a question and therefore needs to include the important information from the question. Following are a few steps to model to help them acquire the information needed for their opening:

1. When responding to an open response question, there should be a minimum of two sentences for each part of the question.
2. The first sentence should restate the question and include the answer.
3. The subsequent sentence(s) should explain the process taken to answer the question.

I have found that this step is difficult for students at first, but with more practice, it becomes second nature.

Modeling the Rest of the Response

To help students with the overall process of drafting, you can use Figure 6.4, which is my model response in an annotated format. Place the figure on an overhead transparency and walk the students through the important

Annotated Final Draft Model Part I

Name _____

Date _____ Class _____

Reminder!
Answer and label
each part.

Task:
- Answer all parts of the question.
- Answer in an organized and focused manner.
- Include appropriate details (for example, diagrams, charts, tables, definitions).
- Use math vocabulary to the best of your ability.
- Complete computations carefully and accurately.
- Explain the main ideas in your writing.
- Demonstrate your best mechanics and grammar.
- Include all stages of the process.

Question:

A group of students recorded the attendance data for their homeroom over two weeks. The results are shown in this table.

Homeroom Attendance Data

Date	Students Present (Total 21 students)
December 5	19
December 6	21
December 7	20
December 8	19
December 9	18
December 12	17
December 13	19
December 14	15
December 15	16
December 16	20

Use your math vocabulary!

A. Create a table using the above information that will show the attendance data as a fraction and as a percent.

B. Create a stem and leaf plot of the attendance data using the percentages.

C. What is the mode of the attendance data?

D. What is the mean of the attendance data?

E. What is the median of the attendance data? Show or explain your work.

Figure 6.4.   Annotated final draft model (Part I).

Annotated Final Draft Model Part II

Response A.

Date	Students Present (Total 21 students)	Fraction of students present	Percent of students present
December 5	19	19/21	90%
December 6	21	21/21	100%
December 7	20	20/21	95%
December 8	19	19/21	90%
December 9	18	18/21	86%
December 12	17	17/21	81%
December 13	19	19/21	90%
December 14	15	15/21	71%
December 15	16	16/21	76%
December 16	20	20/21	95%

➡ **Notice how the opening sentence restates the question.**

The table above shows the attendance **data** as **fractions** and as **percents**. *I found the **fraction** by recording the number of students present over the total number of students.* The number of students present is the **numerator** because it is the number of parts of the whole that are being considered. The total number of students is the **denominator** because it is the number of parts that make up the **whole**. *I found the percent of students present by **dividing** the **numerator** by the **denominator** and changing the **quotient** to a **decimal**.* My **quotients** were **decimals**. I know that .90 is read ninety hundredths, which is equal to 90%.

Example:
$19 \div 21 = .904761$ which when rounded to the nearest tenth is .90
$.90 = 90/100 = 90\%$

- **Math vocabulary is in bold**
- *Thinking processes are in italics*

B.

90	71
100	76
95	81
90	86
86	90
81	90
90	91
71	95
76	95
95	100

Figure 6.4. Annotated final draft model (Part II).

Annotated Final Draft Model Part III
Homeroom Attendance Percentages

Stem	Leaf
7	16
8	16
9	00155
10	0

Opening sentence restates question.

B. I created a stem and leaf **plot** of the attendance **percentages**. *To do this I first listed the **data** from **least** to **greatest**. Next, I used the numbers in the **tens** or **hundreds** place as my stem and the numbers in the ones place as my leaves.*

C. The **mode** of the students present is 90%. **Mode** is the **value** that appears most often in the **data**. 90% appears three times.

D. The **mean** of the attendance data is 87%. **Mean** is the **average** of a set of numbers. *To find the **mean** I found the **sum** of the attendance **percentages** and **divided** by the number of **percents**.*

```
  90
 100          874 ÷ 10 = 87.4
  95
  90          87.4 rounded to nearest whole number is 87
  86
  81
  90
  71
  76
+ 95
─────
 874
```

E. The **median** of the attendance **data** is 90%. The **median** is the middle **value** in a list of **statistics** ordered from **least** to **greatest**. *To find this I listed the **data** from **least to greatest** and found that 90 is the **percentage** in the middle.*

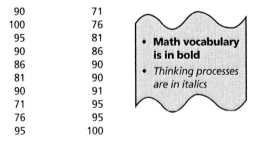

90	71
100	76
95	81
90	86
86	90
81	90
90	91
71	95
76	95
95	100

- **Math vocabulary is in bold**
- *Thinking processes are in italics*

Figure 6.4.   Annotated final draft model (Part III).

parts of the response. Again, as students begin to produce responses, find exemplary parts of students' work and place on the overhead projector as you verbally explain why each part is well done.

REVISING AND EDITING THE ROUGH DRAFT

When the rough draft is completed, the response needs to be revised and edited.

During *revision*, the writer is improving:

- the organization of the piece.
- appropriate use of math vocabulary.
- sentence structure.
- inclusion of appropriate details such as diagrams, equations examples, charts, graphs, definitions, formulas, tables.
- inclusion of supporting details in words.
- inclusion of details from the question.

  During the revision stage, it is often useful to use a peer revision session asking students to examine each other's responses for the salient parts. In addition, it is usually best to conduct two lessons to help students revise for (a) inserting appropriate math vocabulary, and (b) checking to be sure that each part of the question is completed.

Following are the two strategies I model using a student's response on the overhead:

Revision Strategy for Inserting Math Vocabulary

1. Circle all nouns and verbs.
2. Decide if you know a math word that would be more specific.
3. Replace orginal words with more specific math vocabulary.

Revision Check for Question Completion

1. Reread the question and response.
2. Ask yourself, "Does the response completely answer the question?"
   - Does the first sentence answer the question and include part of the question?
   - Does the second tell the process steps you took to answer the question?
   - Is your thinking included?
   - Did you include all computation and math work?
3. If any of the above is missing, revise accordingly.

Also, at this stage, encourage students to edit for grammatical, mechanical, and spelling errors.

PUBLISHING AND SHARING THE FINAL DRAFT

Before students share their responses, they should complete a final editing including polishing their tables, graphs, and charts. You may then wish to arrange some means for them to share their responses with classmates, peers from other classes, and their families. The act of public sharing helps students to understand, in a concrete way, the concept of writing for an audience. Finally, students can learn from other students' works how to refine their future responses.

EVALUATING THE FINAL DRAFT

The rubric I use is included in Appendix A and is designed to help your students understand the performance criteria for a mathematical open response question. While the students are completing their responses, they should refer to the rubric as a guide. When they complete their responses, have them self-evaluate and make revisions according to the rubric. Finally, you can score them using the rubric and convert the score to a letter grade if necessary.

CHAPTER 7

THE REFLECTIVE ESSAY

A Guide to Personal Discovery

Audrey G. Rocha

THE NATURE OF THE GENRE

A reflective essay is a genre in which authors take time to personally reflect on events, people, places, and/or ideas that affect them. Ultimately, the purpose of the reflective essay is to lead to an author's personal discovery and help the author become aware of the deeper meaning associated with an event or an encounter (San Diego State University, n.d.).

It is important to teach the reflective essay because it promotes middle school students' understanding of how world events influence their own lives. It is especially relevant in the content area of social studies, history, and/or science as students can track world, national, or cultural events that have made an impact on their lives and articulate how those events may or may not have changed them. One of the outcomes is that during the act of writing, hopefully your students will "transform" their thinking about an event or a personal encounter (Bereiter & Scadamalia, 1987).

The best reflective essays use a subtle tone that addresses the person, place, idea, or event on which the author is reflecting. Usually a reflective essay does not reveal and state the author's opinion until the end of the essay; instead

Teaching Writing Genres Across the Curriculum, pages 91–103
Copyright © 2006 by Information Age Publishing

the author can embed several hints in the piece that point toward the author's views and final reflections (San Diego State University, n.d.).

To help guide you and your students into this type of writing, it is important to know the steps involved in a reflection. They include:

1. Author has an experience.

2. Author recognizes that this experience has had some kind of influence on his/her life.

3. Author thinks about what specific ways the experience affected him/her.

4. Author decides how this experience has changed his/her ideas about people, events or life in general.

5. Author remembers enough of the important details surrounding the experience to help write the essay.

Embedded throughout this chapter are ways to model and provide practice for your students in each of these important steps.

INTRODUCING THE GENRE: USING A MODEL ESSAY TO EXEMPLIFY THE GENRE

As suggested in Chapter 1, the best way to orient students to a new writing genre is to provide them with a model essay. This helps students "picture" the genre and assists them as they think about their own topic selection and reflection.

To start your teaching, have your students read the following model essay. While reading, ask them to think about what makes this genre unique. Your goal in this first teaching step is to have students examine the model essay isolating the components and elements that make this genre unique.

Model Essay: Terrorism's Answer

Natural disasters strike, lives are lost, and people ask, "What can I do to help?" When the disaster is of the manmade kind, the question seems that much more important. Although the word terrorism is relatively new, the concept is not. Terrorism has existed since man took up arms against each other. When on September 11, 2001 planes crashed into one of the Twin Towers in New York, everyone sadly looked on believing they were observing a terrible accident. Two minutes later another plane struck the other tower and people were incredulous, "Could it really have been two accidents? Is it coincidental?"

People tuned into national and local television stations to see the footage being played over and over again. People who got out of the buildings were in shock. The nation was unsure of what was happening or of what to do. Then the Pentagon was hit. Finally, more reports came in about a plane headed for the White House that was somehow heroically brought down by passengers who banded together to fight back. Everyone aboard was lost, including the terrorists who overtook the plane. It was too devastating to comprehend.

Desperately I called my family. I was sure this was the end. Armageddon. My mom couldn't come home from work but assured me everything was okay and that I should stay in school. I was petrified. Watching the news all afternoon was both mesmerizing and dreadful. Replays of the day seemed like a movie being run over and over, but it wasn't. It was real life, a page of history, being played out right in front of us. These were real people, not actors in a mega-hit movie. I lost hope that any survivors would be found, including the fireman and police officers that were the first to respond to try to help people who were stuck in the buildings. Incredulous as it was, people were rescued from the rubble. Unreal stories of how people helped each other to get out of the buildings, how a stairway became a safe-haven, and stories of survival that were better than any I had ever read about.

My school organized a drop off spot for people in our town to bring goods desperately needed by the volunteers who left their jobs to help NYC dig out of the mess. The generosity of my town was stunning. Three truckloads were sent off filled with supplies. Celebrities later held a telethon to raise money for the families of the victims. The charity of the American people was awesome. Later, the President requested that at the designated time, everyone should leave their houses to light a candle in support of the thousands who were lost. As we stepped out of our houses to take part in this ritual, I noticed some of my neighbors. Some of them who never even spoke to each other were crying and hugging. It was then that I realized that in times of trouble people need to lean on each other. It is only in this act of support and strength that we can get through any disaster, natural or manmade.

Elements of the Genre

To guide your debriefing of the elements of the genre, Figure 7.1 lists the main elements that make this genre exceptional. In addition, as in all essays, you want to be sure your students' essays are well organized, have an introduction to the experience that engages the reader, include a body of

---

Elements of a Reflective Essay

1. The piece is written in the first person voice.
2. The body of the paper hints at the author's opinion.
3. The author uses a subtle and reflective tone.
4. The piece should incorporate reflective language: "I think about"; "I wonder"; "I'm interested in knowing."
5. There is no "moral to the story."
6. The author's opinion is included in the concluding paragraph; it may be stated directly or simply hinted.
7. The reflective essay is based on the author's own experience; it is through this experience that the author derives meaning.

Figure 7.1.   Elements of a reflective essay.

evidence that supports the topic's significance, and presents a conclusion that reflects why the subject is important to the author. (Note: Appendix B contains full-size figures you can reproduce to make handouts and transparencies for your class.)

In a reflective essay, as with other pieces of writing, the purpose for writing and the audience is clear and consistent. Though often reflection is written for the author to investigate his own feelings, he is still writing for an audience. The focus needs to be determined and maintained throughout the piece.

Finally, understanding of the English language must be exhibited. That is, spelling and grammar need to be accurate unless use of the vernacular is needed to enhance the author's writing.

Once students have debriefed their understanding of what a reflective essay looks like, it is time to move on to topic selection.

PLANNING STEP 1: SELECTING A TOPIC FOR THE REFLECTIVE ESSAY

There are three ways in which you can approach topic selection. The first is for you to provide the topic for students. For example, if you are a social studies teacher and are interested in having all students reflect on the September 11, 2001 terrorist attack, you can offer that as a class topic and ask students to think about how that world event affected their lives.

The second topic selection model is for you to determine the broad topic from which your students then choose slimmer topics. Again, you can present a frame according to your content area. For example:

1. Science teachers can ask students to choose a scientific or technological discovery that has impacted their lives.
2. Social studies teachers can ask students to choose a person in history that has impacted their lives in some way.
3. Mathematics teachers can ask students to choose one operation they learned and reflect upon its impact on their daily lives.

Finally, you can teach students to select their own topics. This format works well in language arts classes and is beneficial because students will choose topics that are important to their own lives. Following is a method for teaching open topic selection.

Teaching Students to Select an Initial Topic

The first step in topic selection is to have your students develop a list of possibilities. You can model this step while using a think-aloud approach asking questions such as:

- What happened in my life that I still think about often?
- What particular person or an encounter with a person has changed my life?
- What specific place that I visited has changed my perspective in some way? (e.g., Holocaust Museum)

A topic brainstorm chart is included in Figure 7.2. You can use this chart while modeling, and again, as a handout for students to record their possible topics. Immediately after modeling, have your students take about five minutes to brainstorm any important event, person, or place from their lives.

Brainstorming Topics for the Reflective Essay		
Possible Topics:		
People/Things	**Places**	**Events**

Figure 7.2.   Reflective essay topic selection brainstorm graphic.

Guiding Students to Select a Topic

From the list students generated, you now need to guide them to choose one topic. Remind students to choose a topic that is of the greatest interest to them and their lives. Have them think about whether or not the event, person, or place they chose has made a very important impact on their lives.

PLANNING STEP 2: IDENTIFYING SUPPORTING DETAILS

Next, students will need to determine the details that they will use to support the main topic. In other words, what supporting details will help them develop their essay and come to their conclusions? This is an important step in the process because if students cannot brainstorm supporting details, then they may have to choose another topic. Figure 7.3 has a chart in which students should record their details.

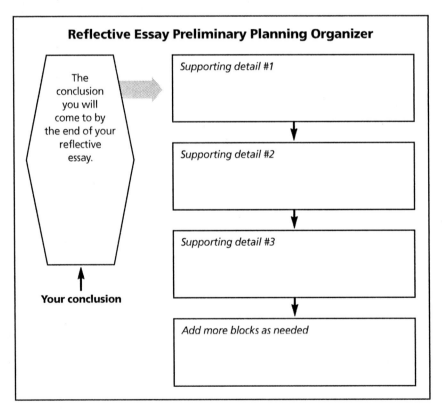

Figure 7.3.   Reflective essay preliminary planning organizer.

In order to model this important step, you can use a simple topic that students all know about or use the one included below which is based on the model essay.

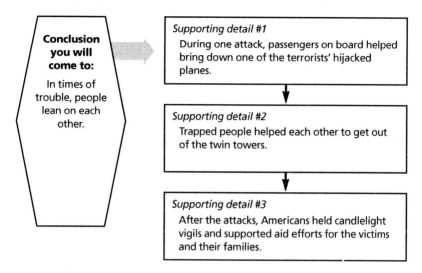

When modeling this step, point out to students that they will have to generate at least three details to support their conclusions. Immediately after students have generated their supporting details, it is important for you to hold teacher conferences to be sure students' supporting details actually support their viewpoint or conclusion. Once you and your young authors are sure the information they generated in this step is valid, it is time for your students to consider their audience.

PLANNING STEP 3: SELECTING AN AUDIENCE

When students write their reflections they are trying to recreate experiences for the reader, therefore, they will need to provide a vivid sense of their experiences. In order to do this effectively they need to consider audience to accommodate appropriate word choice and concept development. The words and the details your students choose are all dependent upon the audience for which the piece is intended.

In order to model for students how to determine an audience, you can introduce the topic by making a transparency of Figure 7.4.

As you guide students through the questions on the audience selection chart, you can help them understand by providing the following details:

- *Why does it matter for whom you write?* Explain how you would write an email to a friend differently from an essay you want published in the newspaper.

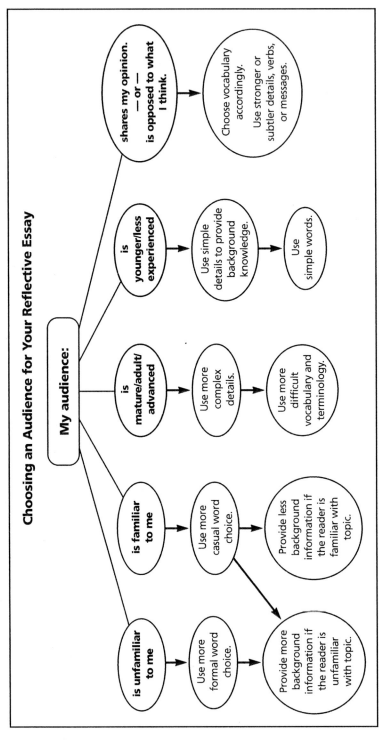

Choosing an Audience for Your Reflective Essay

My audience:

is unfamiliar to me
- Use more formal word choice.
- Provide more background information if the reader is unfamiliar with topic.

is familiar to me
- Use more casual word choice.
- Provide less background information if the reader is familiar with topic.

is mature/adult/advanced
- Use more complex details.
- Use more difficult vocabulary and terminology.

is younger/less experienced
- Use simple details to provide background knowledge.
- Use simple words.

shares my opinion. —or— is opposed to what I think.
- Choose vocabulary accordingly. Use stronger or subtler details, verbs, or messages.

Figure 7.4. Audience selection for the reflective essay.

- *Why does it matter how much my readers know about my topic?* More complex vocabulary, more inferences and in depth explanations can be included if the audience has significant background knowledge. If the reader is new to the topic, clear explanations providing simple background knowledge will lead to a greater understanding.
- *How much background information do I need to supply?* You will need to explain to your students that if their audience is unfamiliar with their topic, then more background information is needed. If the audience is very familiar with their topic, then the details are already part of the readers' prior knowledge.
- *Will the person reading this share my opinion? Be opposed to it?* Finally, students need to project if their readers will share their opinion or be opposed to it. If their final reflection is controversial, then their word choice may have to be more persuasive.

PLANNING STEP 4: DETERMINING FEELINGS AND ADDITIONAL INFORMATION

As a final planning step, you can ask your students to add their feelings, reflections, thoughts, and other descriptive information to compose a well-rounded reflective essay. You can have students add details to their graphic organizers designed in Planning Step 2. The following is an example to help with your modeling.

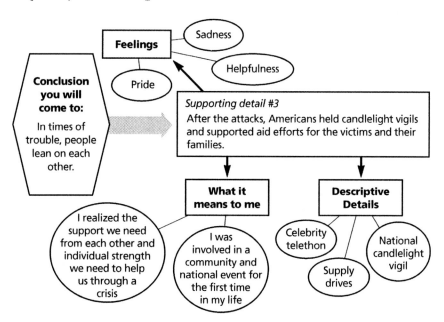

COMPOSING THE ROUGH DRAFT

Your students are now ready to begin writing their first drafts. As students begin to draft, remind them to use their final planning organizer created in the last planning step as a blueprint for drafting. In addition, it may also be helpful to brainstorm how to use a reflective tone in their papers. Encourage them to use word choice that is both tentative and questioning to reveal the reflective process.

Modeling How to Compose the Introduction

As with other genres, it is important that students compose an introduction that entices their audiences to read on. The following information will help you to model how to compose an appropriate introduction for the reflective essay.

1. Engage readers' attention by writing an interesting and gripping lead sentence.
2. In the introduction, include a description of the event that introduces the subject to your readers.
3. Supply the necessary background information according to your audience choice.
4. Prepare your readers for the focus of your essay by hinting at the subject's significance.

Modeling How to Compose the Body

The following information will help you to model how to compose an appropriate body for the reflective essay.

1. Use your graphic organizers to help with the supporting details and organization of your paper.
2. Bring your subject to life by combining narrative and descriptive details with your own thoughts and feelings to make your subject seem real.
3. Include dialogue whenever possible.

Modeling How to Compose the Conclusion

The following information will help you to model how to compose an appropriate conclusion for the reflective essay.

1. Reflect on why this subject is significant to you and possibly to your audience.
2. Reveal your subject's significance and why your feelings about this subject might be significant to the reader.

REVISING AND EDITING THE ROUGH DRAFT

As you may recall from Chapter 1, it is essential to remind your students that revising and editing are two different steps. Revising is part of the ongoing writing process. A piece of work is almost never complete on the first try. There are always ways to improve a piece of writing. Revising and editing are ongoing processes that help writers create a piece of writing that is ever evolving into a work of art.

Before students begin the final revision and editing process, it is recommended that they set their work aside for at least one day. This allows students time to think about their essays and get a fresh look when they begin again. Following is a list of tasks students should consider while revising and editing.

Revising

Ask students to check their pieces for the following:

- Essay begins with a strong introduction that has an enticing lead and clear introduction to the topic.
- Necessary background information is provided.
- The word choice addresses the audience appropriately and is reflective in nature.
- All supporting details, feelings, and reflections are connected to the final viewpoint or conclusion.

Once students have self-revised for the points included above, it may be helpful to ask them to:

- Re-read the essay out loud to a peer to be sure it makes sense.
- Ask peers to confer on further revision ideas.
- Confer with you to finish the revision process.

Editing

The final editing process includes proofreading for grammar and mechanics of writing. The following is a list of a few basic conventions to ask your students to focus on while proofreading:

- Check for capitals: the names of particular people and places.
- Check for appropriate punctuation with a focus on end marks and commas.
- Check the spelling of all words.
- Check subject-verb agreement.
- Comb the piece for fragments and run-ons.

As a final proofreading step, do the following:

- Ask students to participate in an editing peer review.
- Ask students to meet with you to review the final draft.

PUBLISHING AND SHARING THE FINAL DRAFT

As a final writing task, encourage your students to produce a fine finished copy of their essays and share them with their peers and families. To prepare for sharing, ask students to title their essays, making sure the title fits the piece, and prepare to read their essays to the class by practice reading it aloud at least three times to familiarize themselves with the text and decide what inflection they would like to use.

Finally, you can have the class essays displayed around the classroom for classmates and visitors to read at their leisure. The reflective genre is extremely personal and most students take pride in sharing their essays with others.

EVALUATING THE FINAL DRAFT

As suggested in Chapter 1, scoring the writing pieces with an analytic rubric is your final step in genre teaching. A rubric for the reflective essay can be found in Appendix A of this volume, or you can have your students develop a class rubric using the elements of reflection.

Review the rubric with your students so they have an understanding of what is expected of them in their writing. As they develop drafts of the reflective essay, you may use the rubric to evaluate different aspects of the piece. For example, in their first attempt, you may only want to concentrate on having the elements of reflection included eliminating the spelling criteria, etc. Show them how to use the rubric to self-evaluate and make final revisions. With their final draft, have them use the rubric to score all sections of their writing. Finally, you can use the rubric to assess their writing and convert their rubric scores into letter grades with the score conversion chart found at the end of Appendix A.

CHAPTER 8

EXPOSITORY SUMMARY WRITING

Comprehension and Composition

Susan Lee Pasquarelli

THE NATURE OF THE GENRE

Summary writing is an authentic task used in all content area instruction across a wide variety of contexts. Every day we ask our students to summarize what they read, what they learned, or what may have occurred during a school event. In my work in the middle school, I have often confirmed that while we continually ask students to summarize, there is little instruction in how to write a good summary. This chapter is designed to help you to teach one type of summary writing: summarizing expository text.

The summary skill articulated in this chapter will help your students to (a) write a summary of any content area text, (b) write a summary that is suitable for any research paper, and (c) prepare for an oral presentation in any content area. Summary writing is a compelling genre to use in all content areas because it represents two literacy events:

Teaching Writing Genres Across the Curriculum, pages 105–119
Copyright © 2006 by Information Age Publishing

1. Students demonstrate their overall comprehension of the text being summarized.
2. Students demonstrate their expertise in composing a cohesive, explicit summary of the main ideas and salient details of content area text.

In the late 1970s and early 1980s, literacy researchers suggested that summary writing is an exemplary reading comprehension strategy to aid students' abilities to identify and recall specific text information (Brown, Campione, & Day, 1981; Brown & Day, 1983; Kintsch & van Dijk, 1978). Brown and Day (1983) investigated what a good written summary includes and developed the practice of using the following set of rules to guide the written summary.

1. Select a topic sentence from the text or impose one.
2. Delete trivial information that is unnecessary for understanding.
3. Delete redundant information.
4. Substitute subordinate terms with superordinate terms for a list of items. For example, use the word *vegetables* instead of *lettuce, broccoli,* and *asparagus.*
5. Substitute subordinate terms with superordinate terms for a list of actions. For example, use the word *exercising* instead of *lifting weights, running,* and *jump roping.*

Over the years, I have experimented with teaching students to write summaries. I learned that it is essential to impress upon students that writing summaries (as well as taking notes for research) involves two separate literacy events: first, reading for meaning, and second, recording what was learned. Following is a model summary based on a text I chose from a popular science trade book. You can use this model to demonstrate what a good summary looks like as well as how it was composed from information in the original text. The original text excerpt precedes my model summary, which is written using the MLA Style of Research Papers (Gibaldi, 2003) consistent with most middle school language arts programs.

Model Summary

Original Text. The following excerpt is from *AN AMERICAN PLAGUE, The True and Terrifying Story of the Yellow Fever Epidemic of 1793* by Jim Murphy. Copyright © 2003 by Jim Murphy. Reprinted by permission of Clarion Books, an imprint of Houghton Mifflin Company. All rights reserved.

Doctors of that era (1793) believed in what was called vis medica-
triz naturae, the healing power of nature. In other words, the body
took its own measures to rid the humors of poisons and set them in
balance once again; the doctor's job was to coax the body along in
this process.

For the most part, medical treatment was very gentle. Herb teas
were prescribed to break a slight fever. A glass of brandy would help a
restless patient get to sleep.

Of course, some symptoms required slightly more drastic measures
to effect a cure ... Bloodletting, or phlebotomy, was also practiced. In
this procedure, a vein was opened and a small amount of blood was
drawn off in a bowl. With a tad less blood, the theory went, the
remaining blood would flow more freely and normally through the
body.

Bloodletting was an ancient and trusted medical practice that had
been in use for more than 2,500 years. Patients were bled to relieve
headaches, depression, disease, and anxiety. Even a broken bone
would bring out a lance and a bowl. The various symptoms of yellow
fever also called for bloodletting.

My Summary

In 1793, doctors believed in the healing power of nature. They
used gentle procedures, such as teas and brandy. They also used more
drastic procedures such as phlebotomy, or bloodletting, which was an
ancient medical practice. During this procedure, doctors would drain
a small amount of the ill person's blood to hopefully make the
remaining blood flow more freely. Bloodletting was used for a variety
of illnesses including yellow fever (Murphy 59).

WORKS CITED

Murphy, J. (2003). *An American plague, the true and terrifying story of the yellow
    fever epidemic of 1793.* New York: Clarion Books, p. 59.

Elements of the Genre

As suggested in Chapter 1, it is important for students to understand the
nature of the genre and identify the traits or elements that make the genre
of summary writing unique. In Figure 8.1, I have presented the elements of
the genre using middle school-friendly terminology to help your students
conceptualize the genre (Brown & Day, 1983). After students read the origi-

nal text and the model summary, I suggest that you conduct an inquiry activity asking students to identify the elements of the genre. To be sure you have generated all of the genre elements, you can add to the students' list by consulting the elements suggested in Figure 8.1. Appendix B contains full-size figures you can use to make handouts and transparencies for your class.

After students have identified their interpretations of the genre elements, it will be beneficial to put the model summary on the overhead and compare the similarities and differences between the original text and the summary. Figure 8.2 is an annotated summary to help you conduct this part of the lesson.

Elements of an Expository Text Summary

A good written summary...

- Contains a topic sentence that explains what the text is about. The topic sentence should be written in your own words.
- Contains all the main ideas of the text and only the very important details.
- Does not repeat any information.
- Does not include any trivial or unimportant information.
- Uses verbs suggesting a category instead of a list of verbs. For example, if your text is about sports, use the word, *"exercise,"* instead of listing all the types of exercise such as *"running, weightlifting, and jump-roping."*
- Uses nouns suggesting a category instead of a list of items. For example, if your text is about sports, use the word *"equipment,"* instead of *"weights, mats, and exercise balls."*

Adapted from (Brown & Day, 1983).

Figure 8.1.   Elements of a written summary.

Paraphrased the topic sentence from the original text

↓

In 1793, doctors believed in the healing power of nature. They used gentle procedures, such as teas and brandy. ◄——— **Main idea 1**
They also used more drastic procedures such as phlebotomy, ◄—— **Main idea 2**
or bloodletting, which was an ancient medical practice. ◄——— **Important detail**
During this procedure, doctors would drain a small amount ◄——— **Important**
of the ill person's blood to hopefully make the remaining **detail**
blood flow more freely. Bloodletting was used for a ◄——— **Important detail**
variety of illnesses including yellow fever (Murphy 59).

↑

Reduced list of illnesses to a common noun, "variety"

Also, the length of the summary is significantly shorter than the text. The original text = 189 words; the summary = 70 words.

Figure 8.2.   Features of the model summary.

As your students begin to understand the elements a good summary includes (and does *not* include!), it is time to teach them an expository reading comprehension strategy to aid their identification of text ideas. This is an essential first step in the process of writing a summary.

PLANNING STEP 1: IDENTIFYING THE TEXT STRUCTURE OF THE ORIGINAL TEXT

As suggested earlier in this chapter, it is important for your students to understand that writing a summary includes two separate literacy events: reading and comprehending as well as the act of composing. Over the years, I have become convinced that the easiest way to teach students to focus, comprehend, and record material for a summary is to first have them identify the text structure of the expository piece. Researchers on reading comprehension are very clear about the importance of teaching students to identify text structure to aid overall comprehension of text (Brown, Campione, & Day, 1981; Garner, 1987; Meyer & Rice, 1984).

Meyer and Rice (1984) have suggested that there are five ways that text is organized. Students must first be acclimated to these organizational structures before you proceed with teaching how to identify text structure and record ideas from the text. The most common text structures are presented below and are also reproduced in Appendix B for your classroom use.

1. *Classification or Description.* The main ideas are classified and described. For example, if the text were about whales, the information may be organized to describe sperm whales, killer whales, and right whales.

2. *Sequence.* The main ideas are organized sequentially. For example, the text may describe step by step how a baleen whale filters its food.

3. *Comparison/Contrast.* The information is organized to identify similarities and differences among main topics. For example, the text may describe the similarities and differences between whales and dolphins.

4. *Cause and Effect.* The main ideas are organized to identify causes and effects of a certain phenomena. For example, the text may describe the causes of whale disease, or it may describe the effects of an oil spill on a whale population or the causes and effects of the migration of a certain population for whales.

5. *Problem/Solution.* The main ideas are organized by problems and solutions. For example, the text may describe the problems of whale extinction and the solutions scientists are attempting to save a certain whale population.

Teaching Students to Identify Text Structure

In my experimentation with teaching expository text structures, I have established that if students have had no previous instruction, it is best to teach the structures one at a time. I usually begin by teaching the *sequence text* structure because it is one in which students have the most prior knowledge. To begin, I present students with a text that has an overall sequential text structure such as the one found in Figure 8.3.

As I present the text to students, I explain that text structure, or *the ways in which the text is organized,* can be identified on the whole text level (macro), paragraph level and/ or sentence level (Meyer & Rice, 1984). The text found in Figure 8.3 is an example of a whole text level text structure. As students peruse the sample text, I explain that for each text structure, the author usually provides clues, or *signal words*, that indicate the text structure or how the text is organized. For example, the most common signal words used to indicate the sequential text structure are: *first, second, third, next, then,* and *finally* or a *list of dates* (Refer to Appendix B in the summary writing section for a complete list of signal words for all text structures).

PLANNING STEP 2: SELECTING A GRAPHIC ORGANIZER FOR THE SUMMARY

The next step of the process includes modeling for students how to place the ideas from the text into a standard text structure organizer such as those found in Figure 8.4. (Appendix B has a sequential graphic organizer in full-page format that you can photocopy for your students to use during this phase of this lesson).

Usually I just model recording ideas in the first two blocks, and then ask students to work with a partner to identify and organize the rest of the ideas from the paragraph. As students continue with this guided practice, you will notice that what they are scribing will become the main ideas included in the summary. At the end of this exercise, your students' graphic organizers will have a complete picture of the main ideas and salient details such as that included at the bottom of Figure 8.3.

Of course, most information in textbooks does not present information in explicit simple text structures as the sample I have provided. In that case, readers may have to *impose* a text structure to glean the necessary information from text. Imposing a text structure is a bit more difficult for students, but you can coach them to success by practicing on a wide range of text selections written in a wide range of text structures.

Several of the worst oil spills in recent times have been recorded in marine history. In 1997, there were three oil spills in Asia that affected shellfish and beaches. On January 7, in Japan, a Russian tanker leaked 5,200 tons of heavy fuel oil on beaches and threatened shellfish beds. On July 2, also in Japan, a tanker leaked 1500 tons of crude oil onto a fishing ground famous for its seafood. Lastly in 1997, on October 15, a huge tanker, which was carrying 120,000 tons of fuel leaked and coated several smaller islands off Singapore.

From 1998-1999, there were three more significant oil spills in Nigeria and Australia. On January 12,1998, the largest oil spill in Nigeria (40,000 barrels) threatened fish and destroyed fishing nets. In 1999, Australia was affected by two significant spills. The first spill, on June 28, occurred when a faulty pipe coupling caused 270,000 liters of crude oil to spill, damaging beaches and killing marine life. The second occurred on August 3, when a harbor was destroyed while an oil ship was unloading and a breach in the ship caused 80,000 liters of light crude oil to leak ("Snapshot oil spill").

WORKS CITED

Snapshop Oil Spill History, March 8, 2005. Whales Online. Available at: http://www.whales-online.org/

Summary Writing Sequential Graphic Organizer

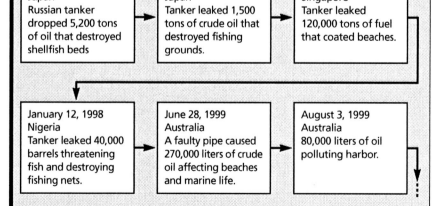

Figure 8.3.   Sample text written in sequential structure.

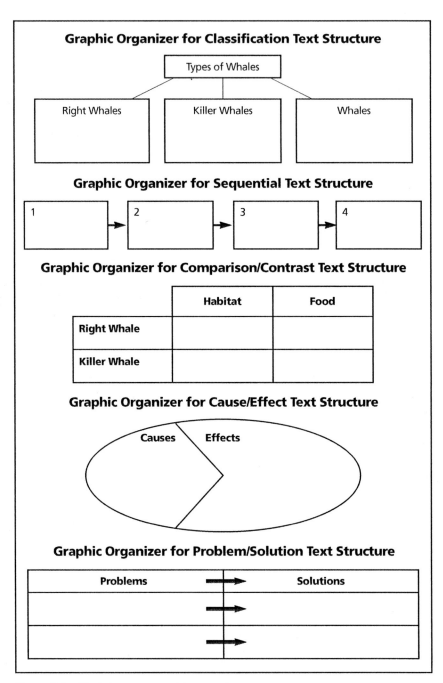

Figure 8.4.   Text structure graphic organizers.

To help you with teaching all five text structures, Appendix B includes a list of signal words, as well as practice texts and graphic organizers for *each* text structure. Again, once you have students practice with the sample texts, have them practice in any content area textbook imposing text structures to identify the important main ideas. Once students have practice recording graphic organizers for each text structure, you can then proceed teaching the composing aspects of the written summary as suggested below.

PLANNING STEP 3: SELECTING OR WRITING THE TOPIC SENTENCE FOR THE SUMMARY

One of the essential steps in writing a summary is to begin with a topic sentence that suggests the contents of the summary. Students sometimes have difficulty composing a sentence that grasps the gist of the entire original text.

To teach this step, you can use the original sequential text (i.e., oil spill) that you and your students used to practice identifying and recording ideas in a sequential text structure (Figure 8.3). Place the original text on the overhead and tell students you will conduct a think-aloud to demonstrate how you determine the topic sentence for your summary. For example, for the sequential information on oil spills, I might say:

> To determine the topic sentence of my summary, I have to think about what the entire summary is about. To help with my composing, I am going to reread the opening of the original text.
>
> Hmm… the text says: "Several of the worst oil spills in recent times have been recorded in marine history." Well, that sounds like a clear thesis statement or topic sentence because the rest of the text is clearly about the worst oil spills in history.
>
> To compose a topic sentence in my own words, I must first understand what the text is mainly about… well, the original sentence is stating that there were several oil spills recently and they are so significant that they are recorded in historical documents. The text then goes on to explain six significant oil spills that took place during the 1990's. Therefore, I can include all that information in my topic sentence. I am going to try to compose my own summary topic sentence using that information. How about this sentence?"
>
> (Write on overhead) *During the late 1990s, there were six significant oil spills in the world that are considered to be historical.*
>
> Hmm… Since this is a summary, I should try to make my topic sentence as clear and concise as possible. I'm going to revise my topic sentence to try to make it more concise. How about this sentence?"

(Write on overhead) *During the late 1990s, there were six historical oil spills in the world's oceans.*

Once you believe students have the basic idea, have them attempt to write a topic sentence for the same paragraph as practice. After sharing topic sentences, you can save a student's exemplary opening topic sentence to use as a model once you have composed the body of the summary draft.

PLANNING STEP 4: COMPOSING THE ROUGH DRAFT WITH THE GRAPHIC ORGANIZER

Model Recording the Main Ideas for the Beginning of the Summary

Explain to students that the topic sentence will be the opening to their summaries. Also make clear that unlike other writing genres, there is not a customary introduction in a summary. To include an introduction will most likely make the summary redundant. Rather, the summary includes just the topic sentence as an opening that leads right into the body of the piece.

Model Recording the Main Ideas for the Body of the Summary

To teach this step, you can use the graphic organizer that you and your students completed earlier on the sequential text (Figure 8.3). Place the graphic organizer on the overhead projector and have a blank transparency ready. You will need to alternate using the graphic organizer and writing the summary on the blank transparency. If possible, having two overhead projectors helps you to complete this step with ease. Again, in order for students to understand your thinking, conduct a think-aloud while you transfer your main ideas from the graphic to the summary draft.

For example, for the sequential information on oil spills, I might say:

To determine the body of my summary, I have to refer back to my graphic organizer to glean the main ideas and important details. The first block says:

January 7, 1997
Japan
Russian tanker
dropped 5,200 tons
of oil that destroyed
shellfish beds

Therefore, the first thing I have to do is take my notes from my graphic organizer and turn them into well-constructed sentences. So I will begin with the date, place, and event and write my first sentence.

(Write on overhead) *On January 7, 1997, a Russian tanker dropped 5,200 tons of oil in an ocean near Japan.*

Hmm… I can revise my writing later so I am just going to continue writing with all the information I have.

(Write on overhead) *That spill devastated the Japanese fish economy because many shellfish beds were destroyed.*

I will continue to determine the body of my summary, by adding information from the second block of the graphic organizer. The second block says:

> July 2, 1997
> Japan
> Tanker leaked 1,500
> tons of crude oil that
> destroyed fishing
> grounds.

Again, using my notes from my graphic organizer, I will turn them into well-constructed sentences.

(Write on overhead) *On July 2, 1997, a tanker dropped 1,500 tons of crude oil in an ocean near Japan. This spill also destroyed fertile fishing grounds.*

After you have modeled the first two blocks of the graphic, have students practice writing the remainder of the body of the summary using the last four blocks included in their graphic organizers. Before they begin practicing, remind your students that the summary can be revised after they have scribed the information onto their rough drafts.

At the completion of the guided practice, it is helpful to have a whole group share of students' rough drafts. At this time, I recommend that you entertain questions or problems concerning *process* as well as *content* that students have encountered while writing their drafts. Typically, I then conclude with scribing a model draft summary on the board or overhead projector.

To complete this teaching step, be sure to explain to students that a customary conclusion is not needed in a summary; in fact, it would probably just repeat the main ideas which is not desirable in a summary format.

REVISING AND EDITING THE ROUGH DRAFT

Revising

Revising summaries requires distinctive revision strategies. Again, it is best to model for students how to conduct this critical revision process. The basic revision steps I suggest are as follows:

1. *Locate and delete trivial information.* Even with the best of modeling, students tend to want to add information that is just not necessary for a summary format. This is not unusual since we tend to encourage the use of elaboration in most other writing genres. To demonstrate this revision step, I often make a transparency of a student's rough draft (with author's permission) to use as a model. I place the transparency on the overhead projector and ask the whole group to help me find information that the student may have included that is just not important. Pay strict attention to elaborate details that are not necessary in a summary.

2. *Locate and delete information that is repeated or redundant.* Again with a student's rough draft, you can model crossing out information that is used twice. Impress upon your students that a summary is meant to be short, concise, and to the point.

3. *Revise to vary sentence beginnings and add transitional phrases.* In my experience, I have found that when students are recording information from a graphic organizer, they tend to use the same sentence beginnings as they compose the summary. For example, in my sample modeling of the oil spill described earlier, both of my sentences begin with the same words. Demonstrate for students how to alter the sentence structure and also how to add signal words or transitional phrases such as: similarly, on the other hand, accordingly, as a result of, etc.

4. *Revise topic sentence to fit the body of the summary and be sure it reflects the overall meaning of the original text.* The last step in the revision process is to ask students to confer with peers to be sure their topic sentences reflect the overall meaning of the text and is an appropriate fit with the newly written body of the summary.

After modeling all of these "new" revision strategies, you will want to remind students to confer with a peer to identify any other information in need of revision such as word choice and overall cohesiveness.

Editing

The editing step is the same as with all other writing pieces. Students should edit their summaries for grammar, mechanics, and spelling, especially of new content specific words. You can use your standard editing checklist to coach students to success during this stage of the process.

PUBLISHING AND SHARING THE FINAL DRAFT

Summaries are simple and easy to polish into final drafts. I often conduct a whole group share of summaries, not necessarily for aesthetic purposes, but rather to create further coaching opportunities. I may reproduce a few exemplary summaries and place them on the overhead pointing out exemplary use of the elements (no trivial details, no redundancy, etc.), or I may post the summaries around the room for other students to use as guides as they continue to hone their summary writing skill. Whatever your venue, as with all genre, it is important for students to share their writing to celebrate success in learning a new genre.

EVALUATING THE FINAL DRAFT

Included in Appendix A is a simple summary rubric you may wish to review with your students while they are involved in composing summaries. The rubric categories are very specific to the summary genre and will remind students during the revision and editing stages of the elements of genre. Providing students with the rubric *before* they finish their summaries will assure that they will work toward meeting the highest performance criteria, especially of the idiosyncratic elements such as deleting trivial information and redundancy. In addition, once students have finished their final drafts, you will be able to score the writing piece and help students to identify the strengths and needs of their first try at summary writing.

SEQUENCE OF WRITING A SUMMARY

Because teaching summary writing is a two-literacy event, I have included in Figure 8.5, an overall summary writing strategy for your students to refer to as they write their first summary independently. It may be helpful to post this strategy in a poster in your room or provide students with a copy for their easy reference. Appendix B includes a full-size model of this figure for your classroom use.

Strategy for Writing Expository Text Summaries

1. **Read** the text once through.
2. **Determine the topic** of the text.
3. **Identify the text structure** (the way the author arranged the ideas). If no text structure is evident, impose one.
4. **Draw an appropriate graphic organizer** to match the text structure you have chosen. For example:

Compare/Contrast

	Habitat	Food
Right Whale		
Killer Whale		

5. **Record the most important information** (main ideas) in the appropriate graphic organizer.
6. **Start drafting the summary** by writing a topic sentence that represents the main ideas of the text.
7. **Use the main ideas and important details** recorded in the graphic organizer to guide writing the remainder of your draft summary.
8. **Revise your draft** by:
   • locating and deleting trivial information.
   • locating and deleting information that is repeated.
   • checking to see if your topic sentence describes the overall meaning of the original text.
9. **Edit your draft** by proofreading for grammar, spelling, capitalization, and punctuation.
10. **Produce a polished final draft**.

Figure 8.5.   Overall strategy for writing summaries.

CONCLUDING REMARKS

As this chapter has indicated, the act of summary writing is a two-literacy event that requires direct instruction in both comprehension and composition strategies. I have attempted to teach summary writing to students who have not had text structure comprehension instruction and found that students' final summaries lack a clear understanding of the original text and include elaborate information not needed in a summary. However, if I provide text structure instruction and practice in identifying and recording ideas, students' very first attempt to write an outstanding summary becomes a positive experience for both the teacher and students.

CHAPTER 9

RESOURCES FOR WRITING ACROSS THE CURRICULUM

Susan Lee Pasquarelli

This chapter offers an annotated list of professional development resources that are available to support your self-study of writing instruction. I have attempted to provide you with a list of the best writing resources that middle school teachers have found useful in their own classrooms.

First, I have included professional development books suitable for all middle school teachers, ranging in topic from books devoted to the overall writing workshop approach to books about very specific writing topics such as teaching grammar through editing. After the professional book listings, I have included publisher's websites so you can easily order books that are of interest to you. Finally, there is a list of support organizations that will aid your progress in teaching writing genre by genre. I hope you find this list of resources useful in your pursuit to provide rigorous, high-quality writing instruction to your middle school students.

BOOKS ABOUT COMPOSING PROCESSES AND WRITING WORKSHOP

Coaching Writing—The Power of Guided Practice by **William Strong, Heinemann, 2001**. *Coaching Writing* is a unique look at what goes on inside writer's workshop as students are working on their pieces. The book is

Teaching Writing Genres Across the Curriculum, pages 121–127
Copyright © 2006 by Information Age Publishing
121

divided into various components of writing, such as: coaching usage, coaching style, coaching voice, etc.

Craft Lessons: Teaching Writing K–8 by **Ralph Fletcher and JoAnn Portalupi, Stenhouse Publishers, 1998.** Included in this book are 78 lessons for teaching particular elements of writing craft such as writing leads, creating voice, structure, supporting detail, setting, mood, and character. A separate section of this text is designed for teaching middle school students.

Just Write! Ten Practical Workshops for Successful Student Writing by **Sylvia Gunnery, Stenhouse Publishers, 1998.** Included in this volume are ten writing workshops teachers can implement in their own classrooms. The workshops include lessons and guided practice in various stages of the writing process.

Lighting Fires—How the Passionate Teacher Engages Adolescent Writers by **Joseph Tsujimoto, Heinemann, 2001.** This is an inspirational and instructional volume that explains Tsujimoto's approach to motivating his students to write both narrative and expository genres.

Motivating Writing in Middle School, **Standards Consensus Series, The National Council of Teachers of English, 1996.** This book is about motivating middle school students to use their own experiences and memories to engage in authentic writing tasks. Included are ways for students to form communities as they peer revise and edit.

Reading and Writing in the Middle Years by **David Booth, Stenhouse Publishers, 2001.** This volume approaches the simultaneous teaching of reading and writing in grades 4-8. Emphasis is on content area reading and making connections to students' lives.

Strategies for Integrating Reading and Writing in Middle and High School Classrooms by **Karen Wood and Janis Harmon, National Middle School Association, 2001.** This is an exemplary volume designed to integrate literacy across the middle school curriculum. Each chapter provides step-by-step guidelines to dissolve boundaries among subject matter. Middle school content area teams will find this book to be a valuable resource for common planning.

Teaching Adolescents to Write: The Unsubtle Art of Naked Teaching by **Lawrence Baines, Allyn and Bacon, 2003.** This book contains lesson plans, evaluation rubrics, and student work samples that describe an intense writing program designed to engage and immerse adolescents in writing.

Teaching Literacy in Sixth Grade **by Karen Wood and Maryann Mraz, Guilford Publications, 2005.** Wood and Mraz have captured a unique look at the literacy transitions from elementary school to middle school. The book's focus is on a sixth grade integrated language arts/social studies program including hands-on strategies for working with diverse learners.

Vocabulary in the Elementary and Middle School **by Dale Johnson, Allyn and Bacon, 2001.** Although this book is not devoted to writing instruction, I included it as a reference since we have emphasized the strong tie between vocabulary instruction and writing instruction. In *Vocabulary in the Elementary and Middle School,* Johnson's premise suggests that vocabulary instruction is integral to all oral and written communication. This is a valuable resource because it provides practical instructional strategies for helping students expand their oral and written vocabularies.

Winning Ways of Coaching Writing: A Practical Guide to Teaching Writing Grades 6–12, **edited by Mary Warner, Allyn & Bacon, 2001.** Warner, a teacher, created a volume dedicated to the middle and high school writing program. Her book includes practical lessons for the beginning writing instructor.

Writing in the Middle Years **by Marion Crowhurst, Heinemann, 2001.** Crowhurst reviews both research and practice in her writing workshop approach to middle school writing. Of particular interest is the focus on developing group interaction during writing instruction and practice.

Writing Our Communities: Local Learning and Public Culture, **edited by Dave Winter and Sarah Robbins, National Council of Teachers of English, 2005.** This unique collection integrates community engagement with writing instruction. As students conduct community based projects, they write about their experiences as well as integrate their research on local culture, history, and environment. This is an excellent resource for teachers wishing to incorporate community involvement into the writing curriculum.

BOOKS ABOUT GENRE STUDY

Blending Genre, Altering Style—Writing Multigenre Papers **by Tom Romano, Heinemann, 2000.** Romano has produced a book that addresses teaching by genre. His work includes how to help students produce multigenre papers and learn various writing strategies related to style.

More than the Truth—Teaching Nonfiction Writing Through Journalism, **edited by Dana Balick, Dennie Wolf, and Julie Craven, Heinemann, 1996.** In this volume, the authors present a unique look at sixth graders who examine changes in their neighborhood through journalism.

The Write Genre—Classroom Activities and Mini-Lessons that Promote Writing with Clarity, Style, and Flash... **by Lori Jamison Rog and Paul Kropp, Stenhouse Publishers, 2004.** *The Write Genre* concentrates on all stages of the writing process and is organized around six genres: personal memoir, fictional narrative, informational report, opinion piece, procedural writing, and poetry.

Untangling Some Knots in K-8 Writing Instruction, **edited by Shelley Peterson, International Reading Association, 2003.** This volume helps to bridge the gap between teachers, administrators, consultants, and researchers on the topic of K-8 writing instruction. There is a section on diversity that addresses ELL and ESL students as well as a section on teaching writing using multimedia and the arts.

BOOKS ABOUT REVISING AND EDITING

Breaking the Rules—Liberating Writers Through Innovative Grammar Instruction **by Edgar Schuster, Heinemann, 2003.** Schuster presents a fresh look at traditional grammar instruction. The book contains "energetic" methods for encouraging students to be independent in their pursuit of grammatical accuracy.

Grammar Alive! A Guide for Teachers **by Brock Haussamen, Amy Benjamin, Martha Kolln, and Rebecca S. Wheeler, The National Association of Teachers of English, 2003.** This grammar guide approaches grammar instruction by describing true classroom experiences. Included are grammar lessons and a review of grammar basics. Also of interest is the authors' focus on ESL issues.

Image Grammar—Using Grammatical Structures to Teach Writing **by Harry Noden, Heinemann, 1999.** The integration of grammar instruction and writing instruction is the focus of this book. Noden suggests that a writer is much like an artist who "paints" images; thus, the title of his book: *Image Grammar.*

Lessons to Share on Teaching Grammar in Context, **edited by Constance Weaver, Heinemann, 1998.** Weaver and other writing researchers and instructors present grammar through writing across the grades/curriculum. This volume includes chapters on sentence composing, ESL writing interventions, editing conferences, and more.

Teaching Grammar in Context **by Constance Weaver, Heinemann, 1996.** We have referred to Weaver's book throughout this volume as one of the seminal works on "new" approaches to grammar instruction. Fifteen years ago, Weaver broke new ground with her assertion that grammar instruction is best taught within the context of editing.

The Power of Grammar—Unconventional Approaches to the Conventions of Language by **Mary Ehrenworth and Vicki Vinton, Heinemann 2005**. This text is grounded in latest research and provides teachers with essential grammar lessons for middle school students.

The Revision Toolbox—Teaching Techniques That Work by **Georgia Heard, Heinemann, 2002**. In this volume, Heard includes revision lessons and conference techniques on three basic revision strategies: words, structure, and voice.

They Still Can't Spell? Understanding and Supporting Challenged Spellers in Middle and High School by **Rebecca Sipe, Karen Reed-Nordwall, Tracey Rosewarne, Dawn Putnam, and Jennifer Walsh, Heinemann, 2003**. This book represents and describes a unique collaboration between teachers and students during their pursuit of spelling interventions. It includes resources to use in your own classroom.

BOOKS ABOUT PUBLISHING AND SHARING

Computers in the Writing Classroom by **Dave Moeller, The National Council of Teachers of English, 2002.** In this volume, Moeller provides teachers with classroom suggestions to facilitate students' expertise in producing polished final writing drafts.

Go Public! Encouraging Student Writers to Publish by **Susanne Rubenstein, The National Council of Teachers of English, 1998**. Rubenstein has created a volume designed to inform middle and high school teachers of publishing opportunities for young authors. Her book includes classroom activities to aid students' confidence to publish their work in a wide market.

Real ePublishing, Really Publishing! How to Create Digital Books by and for All Ages by **Mark Condon and Michael McGuffee, Heinemann, 2001.** Condon and McGuffee have produced a valuable book for teaching students how to create multimedia texts. This book is a step-by-step guide offering the basics on classroom e-publications including digital photography and colorfully printed books for digital sharing within schools and on the Internet.

The Ultimate Guide to Classroom Publishing by **Judy Green, Stenhouse Publishers, 1999.** Publishing students' books is the focus of this volume. It provides concrete ideas on how students can make their own books and establish a writing community within a publishing environment.

BOOKS ABOUT WRITING ASSESSMENT

The Author's Profile: Assessing Writing in Context, **by Teri Beaver, Stenhouse Publishers, 1990.** This book contains rubrics for all types of narrative and expository writing. In addition, there are suggestions for young authors to reach the next level of development.

BOOKS ABOUT WRITING RESEARCH

Adolescent Literacy Research and Practice, **edited by Tamara L. Jetton and Janice A. Dole, Guilford Publications, 2004.** This book suggests that literacy instruction enhances content area learning and fosters student motivation and success. The volume includes sections on teaching content area domains through literacy, teaching adolescents with literacy difficulties, and critical issues in adolescent literacy.

Handbook of Research on Teaching the English Language Arts, **Second Edition, edited by James Flood, Diane Lapp, James Squire, and Julie Jensen, copublished with Lawrence Erlbaum Associates and the National Council of Teachers of English, 2002.** This volume is a must for professional development libraries. Written by prominent researchers in the field of literacy, this handbook offers the latest developments in all aspects of literacy processes. Used often by curriculum developers and teachers, this handbook is helpful to determine best practice K–12 literacy instruction.

Handbook of Research on Teaching Literacy Through the Communicative and Visual Arts, **edited by James Flood, Shirley Brice Heath, and Diane Lapp, Lawrence Erlbaum, 2005.** This handbook is a compilation of the conceptualizations of literacy that include the traditional communicative arts and the visual arts of drama, dance, art, video, and computer technology.

Perspectives on Writing: Research, Theory, and Practice, **edited by Roselmina Indrisano and James Squire, International Reading Association, 2000.** Indrisano and Squire have gathered several of the most prominent researchers on writing instruction to present the latest theory and practice on writing instruction. What sets this volume apart from other research-based books is its practicality for teachers. This is a volume that my graduate students read from cover to cover.

EDUCATION PUBLISHERS' WEB SITES

To order books recommended in this volume, I have included the publisher's Web sites below.

- **Allyn & Bacon** *www.ablongman.com*
- **Guilford Press** *www.guilford.com*
- **Heinemann** *www.heinemann.com*
- **International Reading Association** *www.reading.org*
- **National Middle School Association** *www.nmsa.org*
- **Stenhouse Publishers** *www.stenhouse.com*
- **The National Council of Teachers of English** *www.ncte.org*

PROMINENT LITERACY SUPPORT ORGANIZATIONS

- **International Reading Association (IRA)** *www.reading.org*
  The International Reading Association is a professional organization dedicated to promoting high levels of literacy by (a) disseminating research and practice about literacy, (b) engaging in advocacy to support research that improves literacy instruction, (c) enhancing professional development of reading educators, and (d) improving the quality of literacy instruction. This organization reaches 300,000 educators around the world and offers journals, online journals, conferences, grants, awards, and more. Visit the website to peruse the benefits of joining this worldwide organization.

- **National Middle School Association (NMSA)** *www.nmsa.org*
  The National Middle School Association is the only organization devoted solely to the development of the middle school curriculum and the young adolescent. With 30,000 members worldwide, this association offers the *Middle School Journal* and *Middle Ground* magazine. In addition, they offer publications devoted to middle school topics. The website describes their services and membership benefits.

- **The National Council of Teachers of English (NCTE)** *www.ncte.org*
  Since 1911, NCTE has worked to advance teaching, research, and student achievement in English language arts at all levels. Join this organization to be part of a network of English Language Arts professionals. Attend conferences, receive journals with the latest research and practice, apply for grants, etc. Visit the website to learn more about this organization.

Appendicies

APPENDIX A
Scoring Rubrics

Rubric for Writing a Narrative Account—Chapter 2

	4 Proficient	3 Developing	2 Beginning to Develop	1–0 Not Yet
Interest level	• The lead captures the reader's attention and creates the proper mood • Story engages the reader through the use of effective dialogue and suspense.	• The lead captures the reader's attention • Story engages the reader through some use of dialogue and suspense	• The lead attempts to capture the reader's attention, but is not successful. • Story attempts to engage the reader, but is not successful	• No lead is provided • Story does not try to engage the reader
Content	• Writing shows strong knowledge, experience and/or insight • Includes all elements of the plot: beginning, rising action, peak, falling action, and ending • Complex characters are developed	• Writing shows adequate knowledge, experience and/or insight • Includes most elements of the plot • Characters are somewhat developed	• Writing shows little knowledge, experience and/or insight • Plot is loosely developed • Characters are shallow	• Knowledge and experience is limited or unclear • The plot is difficult to follow or understand • Characters show little or no development
Organization	• Writing has a strong beginning, middle, and end and is organized well.	• Writing shows a clear attempt at organization but some revision is needed	• Writing is loosely organized	• Writing is disorganized

	4 Proficient	3 Developing	2 Beginning to Develop	1–0 Not Yet
	• Story stays "on track"	• Story mostly stays "on track"	• Story sometimes swerves "off track," interfering with meaning	• Story is frequently "off track," interfering with meaning
Style and Fluency	• All of the ideas are clearly expressed • Writing contains consistent and much use of sensory details • Writing is fluent and uses clear transitions	• Most of the ideas are clearly expressed • Writing contains some sensory details, but more are needed • Writing is generally fluent, with some use of transitions	• Some of the ideas are clearly expressed • Writing contains little sensory detail • Fluency and transitions are weak	• Many of the ideas are difficult to understand • Writing does not contain sensory details • Writing is not fluent, and transitions are lacking
Language Mechanics and Spelling	• Writing contains no errors in mechanics and spelling	• Writing contains a few errors in mechanics and spelling	• Writing contains many errors in mechanics and spelling	• Writing is unintelligible
Writing Process	• All stages of the writing process were followed • Multiple drafts show substantial growth through revisions	• Most stages of the writing process were followed • Multiple drafts show some growth through revisions	• Some stages of the writing process were followed • Multiple drafts show little growth through revisions	• The writing process was not followed • No revisions to original draft were made

Rubric for Writing a Persuasive Essay—Chapter 3

	4 *Exceeds Standard*	3 *Meets Standard*	2 *Nearly Meets Standard*	1–0 *Below Standard*

Content and Elements of Genre	• Introductory paragraph includes a *well crafted*:
	  • hook sentence or two that provides background information
	  • question that poses the argument
	  • thesis statement that reflects the writer's opinion and grabs the reader's attention
	  • list of the three general arguments, but not explained.
	
	• The body:
	  • includes a strong and direct topic sentence in each paragraph
	  • each argument uses evidence and scenarios, which strongly persuade the reader.
	
	• The conclusion restates the thesis in different words, yet an imaginative way.
		• Introductory paragraph includes a fairly well written:
		  • hook sentence or two that provides background information
		  • question that poses the argument
		  • thesis statement that reflects the writer's opinion and grabs the reader's attention
		  • list of the three general arguments, but not explained.
		
		• The body:
		  • includes an adequate topic sentence in each paragraph
		  • each argument uses some evidence and scenarios, which persuade the reader.
		
		• The conclusion restates the thesis in different words.
			• Introductory paragraph is missing two or more of the following elements:
			  • hook sentence or two that provides background information
			  • question that poses the argument
			  • thesis statement that reflects the writer's opinion and grabs the reader's attention
			  • list of the three general arguments, but not explained.
			
			• The body:
			  • needs revision of topic sentences
			  • each argument needs revision of evidence and scenarios, which persuade the reader.
			
			• The conclusion needs revision and restatement of the thesis.
				• No introductory paragraph.
				
				• The body has no evidence to support the three general arguments.
				
				• There is no concluding paragraph.

	4 Exceeds Standard	3 Meets Standard	2 Nearly Meets Standard	1–0 Below Standard
Style	• Vocabulary used is above grade level • Overall composition flows in a cohesive manner.	• Vocabulary used is appropriate to grade level. • Overall wording is well done and easy to follow.	• Vocabulary used is generally below grade level. • Overall wording does not flow well.	• Vocabulary used is too juvenile for the grade level. • Overall wording makes the essay extremely difficult to follow.
Grammar and Mechanics	• Contains *no* errors in the conventions of the English language (grammar, punctuation, capitalization, spelling). • MLA citations are accurate.	• Contains few errors in the conventions of the English language (grammar, punctuation, capitalization, spelling). • MLA citations have some slight errors.	• Contains many errors in the conventions of the English language (grammar, punctuation, capitalization, spelling). • MLA citations have multiple errors.	• Contains serious errors in the conventions of the English language (grammar, punctuation, capitalization, spelling). • MLA citations are not included.

Writing Process	• Student has handed in *all* of these items:
	  • topic selection web
	  • audience selection web
	  • graphic organizer
	  • drafts w/ self revision and peer revision
	  • final draft
	  • shared story with the rest of the class
	
	• Writing has shown exemplary growth from draft to draft.
		• Student has handed in *all* of these items *except for one*:
		  • topic selection web
		  • audience selection web
		  • filled in graphic organizer
		  • drafts w/ self revision and peer revision
		  • final draft
		  • shared story with the rest of the class
		
		• Student has shown adequate growth from draft to draft.
			• Student is missing two or more of the following:
			  • topic selection web
			  • audience selection web
			  • filled in graphic organizer
			  • drafts w/ self revision and peer revision
			  • final draft
			  • shared story with the rest of the class
			
			• Student has shown little growth over the course of the drafts
				• Student did not hand in any of the steps of the writing process.
				
				• Student has shown *no* growth over the course of the drafts.

Rubric for Writing a Feature Article—Chapter 4

	4 *Exceeds Standard*	3 *Meets Standard*	2 *Nearly Meets Standard*	1–0 *Below Standard*
Content	• Writing contains highly detailed and accurate information that matches the purpose of writing. • Vivid word choice shows clear understanding of topic • Uses information from more than three sources	• Writing contains accurate information that matches the purpose of writing • Word choice shows basic understanding of topic • Uses information from at least three sources	• Writing contains some information that matches the purpose of writing • Word choice shows some understanding of topic • Uses information from at least two sources	• Little or no information or information does not match the purpose • Word choice does not show understanding of topic • Fewer than two sources used
Organization	• Very well-organized; text structure appropriate for topic • Clear transitions are used • Outstanding use of text features • Strong lead and closing	• Organized; text structure appropriate for topic • The transitions are mostly clear • Adequate use of text features • Adequate lead and closing	• Weak organization or text structure does not match topic • Some use of transitions • Some use of text features • Weak lead and/or closing	• Poorly organized or no text structure • No transitions • Poor or no use of text features • No lead and/or closing
Sentence Structure and Conventions	• Well-developed sentences with good variety in writing • Few or no errors in spelling, grammar, or punctuation	• Most sentences well-developed with some variety in writing • Some errors, but doesn't interfere with meaning	• Some run-on or incomplete sentences with little variety in writing • Several errors that make writing unclear	• Many run-on or incomplete sentences with no variety in writing • Errors interfere with readers' understanding.
Writing Process	• All stages of the process are included • Graphic organizers complete and detailed • Significant growth from draft to draft	• All stages of the process are included • Graphic organizers complete • Shows adequate growth from draft to draft	• Most stages of the process are included • Incomplete graphic organizers • Shows some growth from draft to draft	• Few or no stages of the process are included • No graphic organizers • Shows little or no growth from draft to draft

Rubric for Writing a Narrative Procedure—Chapter 5

	4 Proficient	3 Developing	2 Beginning to Develop	1–0 Not at this Time
Narrative Procedure Elements	• Purpose is clearly stated • Purpose is maintained throughout the paper • A clearly defined audience is addressed and maintained throughout • All relevant information is included • All unnecessary information is avoided • Relevant graphics are included	• Purpose is stated but not clearly • Purpose is maintained throughout most of the paper • A defined audience is addressed and maintained • Most relevant information is included • Most unnecessary information is avoided • Graphics are included	• Purpose is unclear • Purpose is maintained through only part of the paper • The audience is vague and readers are inconsistently addressed • Some relevant information is included • Some unnecessary information is avoided • Irrelevant graphics are included	• Purpose is not stated • Purpose is not maintained in any part of the paper • The audience is not defined at all • Very little relevant information is included • Too much unnecessary information is included • No graphics are included
Writing Process	• All topic selection procedures were followed • All purpose and audience selection procedures were followed. • All graphic organizers are complete • Clear development from draft to draft	• Most topic selection procedures were followed • Most purpose and audience selection procedures were followed. • Most graphic organizers are complete • Evidence of some development from draft to draft	• Some topic selection procedures were followed • Some purpose and audience selection procedures were followed. • Some graphic organizers are complete • Very little evidence of development from draft to draft	• No topic selection procedures were followed • No purpose and audience selection procedures were followed. • No graphic organizers are complete • No development from draft to draft
Style	• Exemplary and strong explanations • A strong author's voice	• Clear explanations • A visible author's voice	• Explanations are slim but evident • A weak author's voice	• No explanation was used to help reader • No author's voice

Rubric for Writing a Narrative Procedure—Chapter 5 (Continued)

	4 Proficient	3 Developing	2 Beginning to Develop	1–0 Not at this Time
Writing Conventions	• All sentences have proper structure • Very few spelling errors (3 and under) • Very few punctuation and capitalization errors (3 and under) • Extensive variety of simple, compound and complex sentencesv • Good variety of sentence beginnings	• Most sentences have proper structure • Few spelling errors (4–5) • Few punctuation and capitalization errors (4–5) • A good variety of simple, compound and complex sentences • Some variety of sentence beginnings	• Some sentences have proper structure • Several spelling errors (6–7) • Several punctuation and capitalization errors (6–7) • Little variety of simple, compound and complex sentences • Little variety of sentence beginnings	• Very few sentences have proper structure • Multiple spelling errors (more than 7) • Multiple punctuation and capitalization errors (more than 7) • No variety of simple, compound and complex sentences • No variety of sentence beginnings
Writing Organization	• Introduction, body and conclusion are clearly delineated • Introduction includes the purpose and the topic of the paper • All steps are in a logical and correct order • Clear transitions exist between all steps • Conclusion wraps up the entire paper	• Most of the introduction, body and conclusion are clearly delineated • Introduction includes the purpose and parts of the topic of the paper • Most steps are in a logical and correct order • Clear transitions exist between most steps • Conclusion wraps up most of the paper	• Some delineation between introduction, body and conclusion • Introduction includes the purpose but none of the topic of the paper • Some steps are in a logical and correct order • Clear transitions exist between some steps • Conclusion wraps up some of the paper	• No delineation between introduction, body and conclusion • Introduction is vague and does not include the purpose and the topic of the paper • Very few steps are in a logical and correct order • Clear transitions exist between very few steps • Conclusion wraps up little of the paper

Rubric for Responses to Open-Response Questions in Math—Chapter 6

	4 *Proficient*	3 *Developing*	2 *Beginning To Develop*	1 *Not Yet*
Is the question answered completely?	• All parts answered completely • All parts are labeled	• All parts answered but some not complete • Most parts are labeled	• Not all parts are answered. Parts that are answered are complete • Few parts are labeled	• Not all parts are answered. Parts that are answered are not complete • No parts are labeled
Is my work organized and focused?	• Work proceeds logically from one step to the next • Work is easy to read and understand • Separate parts of the work are labeled.	• Most of the work has logical connections • Work is understandable but difficult to read • Some parts of the work are labeled	• Few logical connections in the work. • Work is readable but difficult to understand • Only one part of work is labeled	• No logical connection between ideas • Difficult to read and understand. • Difficult to tell the difference between parts of the question
Does my work contain appropriate details? (Diagrams, equations, examples, charts, graphs, definitions, formulas, tables, supporting details in words)	• Many appropriate details in both words and arithmetic add depth to the work	• There are some details—both in arithmetic and words	• There are very few details but they do fit the problem	• Details do not fit the problem or details are not present
Do I use appropriate math vocabulary correctly?	• Math vocabulary is used appropriately and accurately throughout the work	• There is some math vocabulary used, and it is used accurately	• There is very little math vocabulary used, but it is used accurately	• Math vocabulary not accurate or math vocabulary not used at all

137

Rubric for Responses to Open-Response Questions in Math—Chapter 6 (Continued)

	4 *Proficient*	3 *Developing*	2 *Beginning To Develop*	1 *Not Yet*
Are my computations correct?	• All computation is correct	• There are small math errors but the process is correct	• Computing errors interfere with the solution	• There are so many errors that the main idea of the problem is lost
Does my writing show that I understand the main ideas?	• Explanations show that main ideas of percents and the relationship among percents are fully understood by analyzing and computing them in real life problems	• Explanations show that general ideas of percents and the relationship among percents are understood by analyzing and computing them in real life problems	• Explanations show that basic ideas of percents and the relationship among percents are understood by analyzing and computing them in real life problems	• Explanations show ideas of percents and the relationship among percents are minimally understood by analyzing and computing them in real life problems
Is my use of grammar and mechanics appropriate?	• Superior mechanics and grammar	• Adequate use of mechanics and grammar	• Piece needs proofreading for grammar and mechanics.	• Use of grammar and mechanics interfere with readers' understanding
Did I follow the process as instructed?	• All stages of the process are evident with growth shown from draft to draft. • Careful computational corrections are shown	• Most stages of the process are evident and growth from draft to draft is shown • Computational corrections are shown	• Some stages of the process are evident and some growth from draft to draft is shown • Evidence of some computational corrections is clear	• No stages of the process are included or the process is unclear from work given • Computational errors are not corrected

Rubric for Writing a Reflective Essay—Chapter 7

	4 *Proficient*	3 *Developing*	2 *Beginning To Develop*	1–0 *Not Yet*
Reflective Elements/ Style	• Author's opinion/conclusion stated/hinted at end.	• Author's opinion/conclusion needs slight revision to be clear.	• Author's opinion/conclusion is stated/hinted but completely unclear.	• No author's opinion/conclusion stated or hinted.
	• Subtle tone is craftily used throughout the piece.	• Subtle tone is apparent throughout the piece.	• Subtle tone is used but inconsistently.	• The tone is not recognizable.
	• Clear audience is addressed and maintained throughout.	• The audience is clear and somewhat maintained throughout.	• Audience not very clear.	• Audience not defined or addressed.
	• Details support opinion and are relevant and appropriate.	• Details mostly relevant and support opinion.	• Few relevant details to support opinion.	• Details non-relevant or not included.
	• Reader can trace several elements of author's opinion throughout essay.	• Reader can detect many elements of author's opinion throughout essay	• Few elements of author's opinion can be traced throughout essay	• No elements of author's opinion can be traced throughout essay
Process	*All* of the following are included: • Topic selection web • Audience selection • Graphics • Draft to draft improvement • Several drafts/revision (3–4) • Detail selection graphic complete	Few included: (4–6) • Topic selection • Audience selection • Graphics • Draft to draft improvement • Several drafts/revision (2) • Detail selection graphic complete	Some included (2–3) • Topic selection • Audience selection • Graphics • Draft to draft improvement • Several drafts/revision (1) • Detail selection graphic complete	None or few of the important components are included

Rubric for Writing a Reflective Essay—Chapter 7 (Cont.)

	4 *Proficient*	3 *Developing*	2 *Beginning To Develop*	1–0 *Not Yet*
Writing Conventions	• All sentences exhibit proper sentence structure. • Very few spelling errors (2–3) • Outstanding variety of sentence beginnings • Very few punctuation and capitalization Errors (2–3)	• Most sentences maintain proper structure. • Few Spelling Errors (4–6) • A moderate variety of sentence beginnings • Few Punctuation and Capitalization errors (4–6)	• Few sentences maintain proper structure. • Numerous spelling Errors (more than 6) • Little variety of sentence beginnings. • Many punctuation and capitalization errors (7–10)	• Sentence structure inhibits readers' understanding. • Spelling errors interfere with comprehension of piece. • Too many sentences begin the same way. • Punctuation and capitalization is non-existent
Organization	• Paragraphs include several details relevant to topic. • Introduction, body and conclusion are clearly definable. • Paragraph transitions are numerous and appropriate. • Conclusion wraps up paper expertly and appropriately.	• Paragraphs include many relevant details. • Introduction, body and conclusion are defined but need revision. • Paragraph Transitions need slight revision to take reader from one idea to another. • Conclusion wraps up the paper, but needs slight revision to close the essay well.	• Paragraphs contain few relevant details. • Introduction, body and conclusion are not clearly delineated. • There are some paragraph transitions, but much revision is needed to accommodate the reader. • The conclusion needs to be completely rewritten to bring closure to the piece.	• Details fragmented and unimportant. • No delineation between introduction, body and conclusion. • Paragraph transitions are non-existent • There is no conclusion to the piece.

Rubric for Expository Summary—Chapter 8

	4 Exceeds Standard	3 Meets Standard	2 Nearly Meets Standard	1–0 Below Standard
Content	• Summary contains accurate information that matches the original text.	• Summary contains some inaccurate information that does not match the original text.	• Summary contains significant inaccurate information that does not match the original text.	• Summary contains so much inaccurate information, a new graphic organizer must be completed and the summary must be rewritten.
	• Summary contains concise inclusion of all main ideas.	• Summary contains all main ideas.	• Summary contains most main ideas.	• Summary is missing too many main ideas and must be rewritten.
	• Summary contains concise inclusion of all important details.	• Summary contains all important details.	• Summary contains most important details.	• Summary is missing too many important details and must be rewritten.
	• Summary contains no redundant or trivial ideas.	• Summary contains one idea that is redundant or trivial.	• Summary contains a few ideas that are redundant or trivial.	• Summary needs a full revision to delete redundant or trivial details.
Organization	• Very well organized; text structure appropriate for topic.	• Organized; text structure appropriate for topic.	• Weak organization or text structure does not match topic.	• Poorly organized or no text structure.
	• Clear transitions are used to make the summary cohesive.	• Some transitions are used to make the summary cohesive.	• The summary needs revision to include transitions to help with cohesiveness.	• The summary needs complete revision for cohesiveness.

Rubric for Expository Summary—Chapter 8 (Cont.)

	4 Exceeds Standard	3 Meets Standard	2 Nearly Meets Standard	1–0 Below Standard
Sentence Structure and Conventions	• Well-developed sentences with good variety of sentence beginnings. • Few or no errors in spelling, grammar, or punctuation.	• Most sentences are well developed with some variety in sentence beginnings. • Some grammatical errors, but they do not interfere with meaning.	• Some run-on or incomplete sentences with little variety in sentence beginnings. • Several grammar errors that make writing unclear.	• Many run-ons or incomplete sentences with no variety in sentence beginnings. • Grammar errors interfere with readers' understanding.
Writing Process	• All stages of the process are included. • Graphic organizers are complete and detailed. • Significant growth from draft to draft.	• Most stages of the process are included. • Graphic organizers are complete but not detailed. • Shows adequate growth from draft to draft.	• Some stages of the process are included. • Incomplete graphic organizers that led to lack of information in the summary. • Shows little or no growth from draft to draft.	• No stages of the process are included. • No graphic organizers included. • There is only one draft.

Suggested Grade Conversions for Rubric Scores

Scoring Scale Range	Grade Conversion
4.00–3.67	A
3.36–3.33	A–
3.32–3.0	B+
2.99–2.67	B
2.66–2.33	B–
2.32–2.00	C+
1.99–1.67	C
1.66–1.33	C–
1.32–1.00	D
Below 1.00	F

APPENDIX B

Model Essay: Narrative Account

May be reproduced for classroom use only

THE KNOCK ON THE DOOR
by Michele Barlow

The loud thud jolted Samuel out of his chair. He spun his head around and looked at the front door. "It's just the wind, Samuel," said his mother, Mary. "Now please sit down and finish your arithmetic before that candle burns out."

"Yes, Ma," Samuel sighed.

He sat down to finish his work, but he just couldn't concentrate. The wind had been pounding the old door all night. His father, John, had meant to fix its hinges, but he never got around to it.

Five months earlier, in the spring of 1780, Samuel's father had left home to fight with the American Army under the command of General Nathaniel Greene (White 3). He was supposed to be somewhere in North Carolina at the moment helping to chase the British Army north. America had been at war with England for over five years in an attempt to win its independence. Much of the fighting between 1778 and 1780 took place in the South, where the British Army had control over many regions (White 3). Samuel and his mother prayed every night for his father's safe return to their tiny farm in Williamsburg County, South Carolina. The day he left, John told Samuel to look after his mother and help her tend to the farm. He also told Samuel to make him proud. Samuel didn't quite understand what the word proud meant, but he never bothered to ask his father as he hugged him tight and said, "Goodbye."

As Samuel finished his last arithmetic problem, there was another loud rattle against the door. "I know, I know…it's just the wind," Samuel said, as he turned to kiss his mother goodnight.

Teaching Writing Genres Across the Curriculum, pages 145–200
Copyright © 2006 by Information Age Publishing
All rights of reproduction in any form reserved.

BOOM! BOOM! BOOM!

The sound made the hair on Samuel's neck stand up. "Someone's at the door!" he yelled. Mary rose from her chair and whispered to Samuel, "Go up to the loft and hide under your bed. Don't come out until I say so." Samuel nodded and quickly hopped up the ladder to the loft. Meanwhile, Mary picked up a loose floorboard and gently pulled out a long, slim, gray musket. She had not yet needed to use it, but she knew that the person on the other side of the door could be a British soldier looking for food, or a place to sleep…or worse.

BOOM! BOOM! BOOM!

Samuel could feel his heart beating in his chest as Mary slowly released the latch on the door and stepped back, pointing the musket straight ahead. The door flew open and a tall figure stumbled to the floor. Mary dropped the musket and called out, "Samuel, come down here quickly! This man is badly hurt! Help me get him into the house!" Samuel ran toward his mother and the man lying on the floor. There was dark red blood all over the man's clothes and he was moaning loudly, like an injured animal. As Samuel and his mother pulled the man inside, Samuel's eyes widened in horror. The man's jacket was red!

"Ma, he's a Redcoat!" Samuel screamed.

"Never mind that now, Samuel!" Mary shouted back. "Just get me some clean rags and a bucket of fresh water."

Samuel didn't move. He couldn't. He just stood there, his eyes frozen on the enemy lying on the floor in a small pool of blood. Mary told Samuel to go upstairs and wait for her until she was finished. She found the wound on the soldier's right shoulder, and cleaned it with water. Then she poured homemade ointment on the wound and tied a butterfly bandage around it. The soldier looked into Mary's eyes, moaned softly, and then passed out.

The next morning, Samuel awoke to find his mother feeding the soldier a bowl of porridge. He never remembered falling asleep. The last thing he remembered was watching his mother wash the blood off the floor while the soldier rested next to the fire.

"Samuel," called his mother. "I want you to meet Thomas Cooke. He says he was hurt two days ago during a battle at Kings Mountain, just north of here" (White 3). Samuel just stared down at his feet. He didn't really care. He only wanted to know one thing. "Have you ever killed anyone?" he asked in a whisper.

"Yes, I'm afraid I have young man," replied Thomas. He continued to speak. "I want you to know that I am truly grateful for your mother's kindness, and as soon as I am feeling better, I will be on my way." Samuel nodded without looking at the soldier, and then walked into the kitchen. He appeared a few minutes later with a butter sandwich in his hand and offered it to the soldier. "Thank you very much, young man," Thomas said with a smile. "You're welcome," Samuel muttered back.

For the next three days, Samuel spent a lot of time with Thomas. He learned that Thomas had a son named Jacob, who was the same age as Samuel, living at home with his mother in England. Thomas showed Samuel how to play a new game with his marbles, and even helped him with his arithmetic. Samuel almost forgot that Thomas was an enemy soldier. But then the day came when Thomas had to leave.

"I'll always remember your kindness, Mary," Thomas said softly. He put his hand on Samuel's shoulder, "And I cannot wait to tell my son all about you, Samuel."

"Goodbye, Thomas," said Samuel.

As Thomas walked away with his musket in hand, Samuel looked at his mother. She knew that he didn't understand why Thomas had to go back and fight. "Your father would be very proud of you right now, Samuel," she said. Samuel now understood what that word meant.

WORKS CITED

White, D. The American Revolutionary War: Keeping Independence, Part 3: The End and the Beginning. January 29, 2005. Social Studies for Kids. Available at: http://www.socialstudiesforkids.com/articles/ushistory/revolutionarywar3.htm

Elements of a Narrative Account

Lead
The lead is the first sentence of the piece. It attracts the reader to read on.

Sensory Details
Use of sensory details (sight, sound, taste, touch, and smell) makes the story feel as real as possible.

Story Structure
A narrative account is a story woven around factual information, and has a setting, characters, and events that lead up to a climax and a strong conclusion.

Storyline
A narrative account should have a strong storyline with specific narrative action such as dialogue, tension and/or suspense.

Author's Style
A narrative account has a strong author's voice and vivid word choice.

Point of View
A narrative account is either written in first or third person.

Conclusion
The conclusion wraps up the story and suggests a consequence.

May be reproduced for classroom use only.

Broad Topic Web for Narrative Account

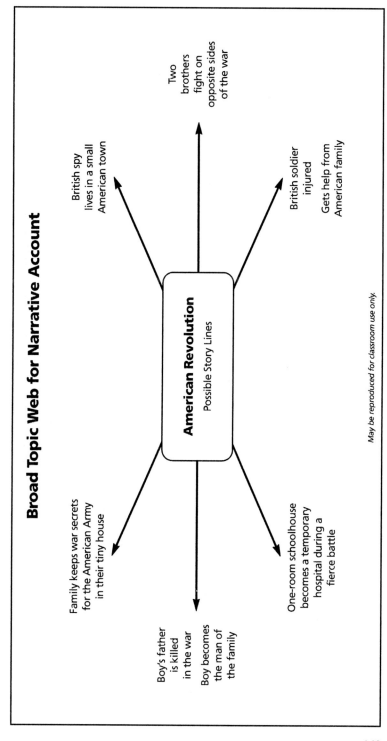

British spy lives in a small American town

Two brothers fight on opposite sides of the war

American Revolution
Possible Story Lines

British soldier injured

Gets help from American family

Family keeps war secrets for the American Army in their tiny house

One-room schoolhouse becomes a temporary hospital during a fierce battle

Boy's father is killed in the war

Boy becomes the man of the family

Narrow Topic Web for Narrative Account

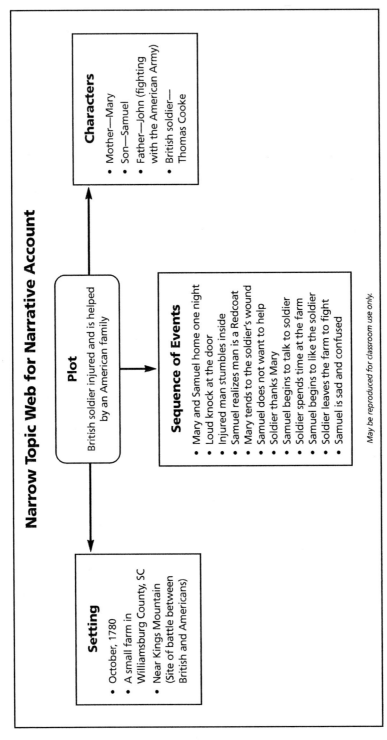

Setting

- October, 1780
- A small farm in Williamsburg County, SC
- Near Kings Mountain (Site of battle between British and Americans)

Plot

British soldier injured and is helped by an American family

Characters

- Mother—Mary
- Son—Samuel
- Father—John (fighting with the American Army)
- British soldier— Thomas Cooke

Sequence of Events

- Mary and Samuel home one night
- Loud knock at the door
- Injured man stumbles inside
- Samuel realizes man is a Redcoat
- Mary tends to the soldier's wound
- Samuel does not want to help
- Soldier thanks Mary
- Samuel begins to talk to soldier
- Soldier spends time at the farm
- Samuel begins to like the soldier
- Soldier leaves the farm to fight
- Samuel is sad and confused

May be reproduced for classroom use only.

Determine the Audience for Your Narrative Account

In order to make writing your narrative account easier, complete the three statements below. Then keep this sheet next to you when you begin writing to help you determine your choice of language and how much description you need to provide your reader.

Why are you writing this account?

I am writing this account to... (check the phrase(s) that apply):

- ☐ explain something.
- ☐ entertain.
- ☐ share a personal story.
- ☐ narrate a story as an eyewitness to a historical event.
- ☐ describe a historical or scientific event from a character's point of view.
- ☐ tell an original tale.
- ☐ make readers feel good.

For whom are you writing this account?

I am writing this account for... (check the phrase(s) that apply):

- ☐ younger children (specify age group: _____).
- ☐ my peers (specify: _____).
- ☐ older children (specify age group: _____).
- ☐ my parents.
- ☐ other family members (specify: _____).
- ☐ the general public (specify: _____).

How much does your audience know about your topic?

My audience is... (check the phrase that applies)

- ☐ not familiar with my topic.
- ☐ somewhat familiar with my topic.
- ☐ very familiar with my topic.

Narrative Account

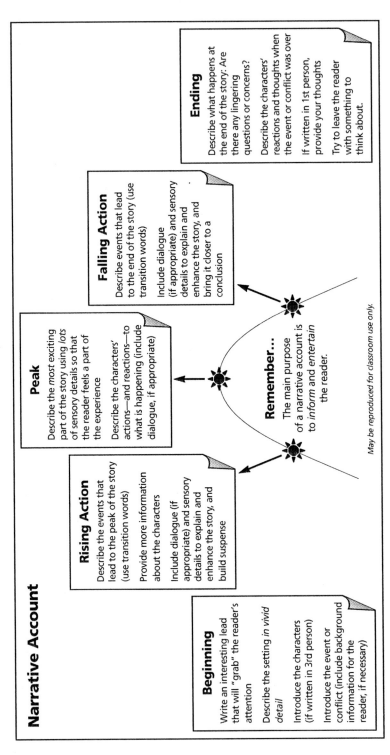

Beginning

Write an interesting lead that will "grab" the reader's attention

Describe the setting *in vivid detail*

Introduce the characters (if written in 3rd person)

Introduce the event or conflict (include background information for the reader, if necessary)

Rising Action

Describe the events that lead to the peak of the story (use transition words)

Provide more information about the characters

Include dialogue (if appropriate) and sensory details to explain and enhance the story, and build suspense

Peak

Describe the *most exciting* part of the story using *lots* of sensory details so that the reader feels a part of the experience

Describe the characters' actions—and reactions—to what is happening (include dialogue, if appropriate)

Falling Action

Describe events that lead to the end of the story (use transition words)

Include dialogue (if appropriate) and sensory details to explain and enhance the story, and bring it closer to a conclusion

Ending

Describe what happens at the end of the story: Are there any lingering questions or concerns?

Describe the characters' reactions and thoughts when the event or conflict was over

If written in 1st person, provide your thoughts

Try to leave the reader with something to think about.

Remember...

The main purpose of a narrative account is to *inform* and *entertain* the reader.

May be reproduced for classroom use only.

Peer Feedback Form

(Narrative Account)

Presenter: _____

Title: _____

TWO PAIRS OF EYES ARE BETTER THAN ONE!

Read my story carefully. When you are finished, please take the time to complete the chart and answer the questions below as thoroughly as you can. Be honest! Your responses will help make my story better. Thank you.

	Needs Improvement	Good	Excellent
The lead captures my attention.			
The story held my interest.			
I feel a part of the experience described in the story.			
The story is clear and organized.			

What did you like **best** about the story?

Describe how I can **improve** the story.

Reviewer's Name: _____   **Date:** _____

Model Essay: Persuasive Essay

May be reproduced for classroom use only

LITTERING: NOT JUST AN ENVIRONMENTAL HAZARD!
by Megan L. Labrecque and Tara A. Fernandes

Littering has been an ongoing problem in our society. Every year, the Environmental Protection Agency educates the general public through various forms of media on environmental hazards ("Trash" 5). Littering is one of them. Although education is provided on a consistent basis, littering continues to be a tremendous problem, affecting the environment, and many other aspects of our lives. Do you feel littering is a problem? Do you feel that littering affects wildlife? Do you feel that littering can be harmful to humans? Do you think littering is economically harmful? I do.

Litter does in fact affect wildlife. Animals can be harmed by the trash that people dispose of improperly. For example, the plastic rings on a six-pack of soda could kill a bird. People go on picnics to the park and beach and think nothing of bringing some soda to drink. Unfortunately, what people may not think of is that when they leave the plastic ring from the soda on the ground, a bird could mistake it for food. If a bird puts one of these in its mouth, it could get its beak tangled or even strangle itself. This is only one small example of how litter affects wildlife ("Trash" 3).

Littering can also be harmful to humans. Many people do not realize that when they are littering, there is a good chance they could be harming themselves in the process. Often, beaches can be forced to close at times during the summer due to water pollution levels and litter being too unsafe for swimmers. "Beach users can be injured by stepping on broken glass, cans, needles or other litter" ("Trash" 3). Are you one of those people who have visited the first aid station because you were barefoot on a beach and were cut on a broken soda bottle? This is a direct consequence of people littering. In addition, people can get sick from drinking contaminated water. Contaminated water could be the result of harmful chemicals, from your litter, absorbing into the ground. Is your drinking water safe?

Lastly, litter is economically harmful. When someone throws a piece of trash on the ground rather than in a receptacle, they are probably not thinking about how much it will cost to be picked up. According to the state of Georgia Department of Transportation ("The Dirty Facts" 1), 15 million dollars has been spent to clean up highway litter in one year. According to the Environmental Protection Agency: "New Jersey spends 1.5 million dollars annually to clean up its beaches" ("Trash" 3). In summary, each year, millions of dollars are spent to clean up after careless people who improperly dispose of their trash. With the economy struggling as it is, money should not have to be used for something that can be prevented.

In conclusion, is littering a problem? Does littering harm wildlife, humans, and the economy? Yes, littering can be harmful; however there are many solutions as to where to dispose trash rather than to turn it into litter. People need to be more educated and less careless. Everyone needs to do his or her part in helping clean up. If you see a piece of trash on the ground, you should bring it to a trash receptacle. If everyone did what he or she could to reduce litter, it wouldn't be such a harmful and expensive problem!

WORKS CITED

Trash In Our Oceans. 2 Feb. 2005. Environmental Protection Agency. 5 Feb. 2005 Available at: http://www.epa.gov/owow/oceans/debris/index.html

The Dirty Facts: Litter in Georgia. 26 Sept. 2003. Georgia Department of Transportation. 3 Feb. 2005 Available at: http://www.stoplittering.com

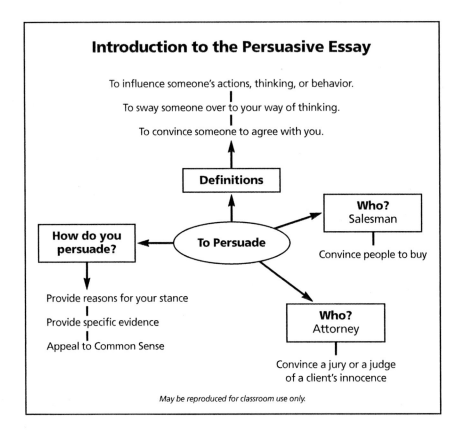

Introduction to the Persuasive Essay

To influence someone's actions, thinking, or behavior.

To sway someone over to your way of thinking.

To convince someone to agree with you.

Definitions

Who?
Salesman

Convince people to buy

How do you persuade?

To Persuade

Provide reasons for your stance

Provide specific evidence

Appeal to Common Sense

Who?
Attorney

Convince a jury or a judge
of a client's innocence

May be reproduced for classroom use only.

Elements of a Persuasive Essay

- The piece has a clear purpose: to persuade the audience to agree.

- The piece addresses a consistent audience.

- The opinion is clearly stated in the opening paragraph.

- Established facts and/or opinions are provided as reasons for the argument.

- Reasons for writer's stance are supported with reasons and evidence so that the reader better understands the issue.

- Background knowledge is provided for those who do not know about the topic.

- Strong persuasive words appropriate to the audience are used.

- The piece includes a conclusion that restates the main ideas and briefly reflects on the importance of the argument.

May be reproduced for classroom use only.

Determining a Purpose and Selecting an Audience for your Persuasive Essay

1. What is my *purpose*? Am I trying to:
- ☐ Inform my readers of things they may not know?
- ☐ Convince my readers of my point of view?
- ☐ Bring about change in my readers' thinking? Persuade?
- ☐ Challenge my readers' thinking about my point of view?

2. Who is my *audience*?
- ☐ Friends?
- ☐ Students?
- ☐ Teachers?
- ☐ Parents?
- ☐ Others?

3. What type of word choice should I use for this type of audience?

4. How hard do I have to work to convince my audience of my point of view?
- ☐ Will they join my side? Will they agree with me? Will they change their opinions?
- ☐ Will they think about what I wrote?
- ☐ Will they consider a new point of view?

May be reproduced for classroom use only.

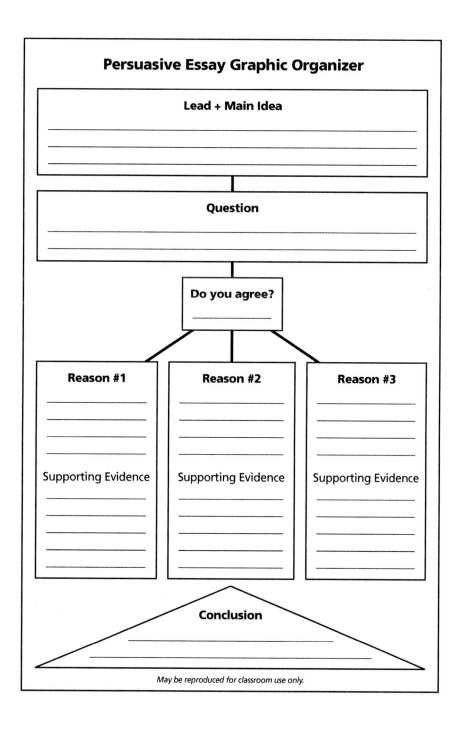

Persuasive Essay Graphic Organizer

Lead + Main Idea

Question

Do you agree?

Reason #1

Supporting Evidence

Reason #2

Supporting Evidence

Reason #3

Supporting Evidence

Conclusion

May be reproduced for classroom use only.

Model Feature Newspaper Article

May be reproduced for classroom use only

WOMEN OF THE MAYFLOWER: WEAK OR WILLFUL?
by Suzanne K. Dunbar

Imagine spending 66 days on a 90-foot wooden ship with 101 other passengers and a crew of 30. As the ship crawls across the Atlantic at an average speed of under 2 miles per hour, strong storms and heavy crosswinds rock it, leaving the ship and its passengers weak. Leaking water drips between the floorboards and soaks the miserable seasick passengers living between the decks. Finally, after being thrown off-course and traveling 2750 miles, land is sighted. An anchor is dropped off the coast of Cape Cod and plans are made to come ashore. The men will gather firewood and explore this new world, while the 18 women onboard will go ashore… to do the laundry!

The Pilgrims knew that the journey across the Atlantic would be long and dangerous, and that they would face even greater hardships when establishing the new colony. Governor William Bradford stated that the men feared the "weak bodies of the women and girls" would not be able to withstand these hardships, and Pilgrim husbands and fathers faced the difficult decision of whether to take their wives and daughters on the voyage or send for them later ("Girls on the Mayflower" 1).

Eighteen women, three of whom were pregnant, and eleven girls made the trip to America, which proved to be as difficult as anticipated. While no women or girls died on the trip itself, the first winter was brutal. The women and girls remained on board the Mayflower for four more months, while the men explored the area and built homes and storehouses. The damp and cramped quarters of the ship became a breeding ground for disease, and only five women survived the first winter. The girls fared better, and actually had a better survival rate than the men and boys. Only two girls died, while 50% of the men and 36% of the boys lost their lives ("Girls on the Mayflower" 1).

Although the survival rate was grim that first winter, the remaining women and older girls proved to be invaluable to the colonists. They cooked, cleaned, and did laundry for the entire colony. They also faced the task of raising the children who were orphaned during this time. While women were expected to be submissive and obey their husbands, the women of Plymouth gained some rights in the new land. They were allowed to buy, sell, and own property, and were given at least 1/3 of their husband's estate, even if the husband did not provide for it in his will. Women were allowed to be a legal witness for a deed or probate document, and they were also given more choice in deciding whom they would marry ("Women on the Mayflower" 1).

Where would America be today without these strong-willed women who first settled here? They not only raised their families in the new world, but also helped build the foundation that enabled later colonists to settle more easily. Today, there are a number of famous people who can trace their roots back to these first Pilgrims. Eight United States' presidents, including George W. Bush, actors such as Clint Eastwood, Marilyn Monroe, and Richard Gere, and the first American in space, Alan Shepard Jr., are all descendants of the Mayflower Pilgrims. This humble group of females, whose first chore in America was to do laundry, provided the quiet strength that allowed this nation to survive and grow to greatness ("Mayflower History" 1).

WORKS CITED

Johnson, C. *Girls on the* Mayflower. 2000. Mayflower Web Pages. 2 Feb. 2005. Available at: http://members.aol.com/calebj/girls.html

Johnson, C. *Women on the* Mayflower. 1998. Mayflower Web Pages. 2 Feb. 2005. Available at: http://members.aol.com/calebj/women.html

Johnson, C. Home page. 2005. MayflowerHistory.com. 2 Feb. 2005. Available at: http://www.mayflowerhistory.com/index.php

Elements of a Feature Newspaper Article

Lead   This introduces the topic and entices the reader through vivid word choice. A lead can start in a number of ways, such as a question, a quote, a startling fact, an anecdote, or a description that sets a scene.

Angle   This is the point of view or perspective from which the topic is explained. Writers must choose the focus of their articles and convey their views to others.

Factual Information Regardless of the topic, factual information must support the writer's views and ideas. The writer may use examples, stories, quotes from experts or even everyday people, interviews, or statistics.

Organizational Structure The writer must choose a text structure to present information, such as compare/contrast, cause/effect, sequential, problem/solution, different perspectives, or the pros and cons of an issue.

Author's Craft   Word choice, print features, and text features, such as charts, graphs, lists, maps, bulleted information, pictures, and time lines, all serve to clarify ideas.

Closure   The closing wraps up the writer's final thoughts about the topic.

Topic Selection for a Feature Newspaper Article

List some topics you are interested in and have some knowledge about:

1. _____

2. _____

3. _____

4. _____

5. _____

I know...	*I wonder...*

Possible resources:

_____

_____

_____

_____

_____

_____

_____

May be reproduced for classroom use only.

How to Choose a Purpose and Audience for a Feature Newspaper Article

My topic is: _____

First, ask yourself, what is my purpose for writing?

- To notify?
- To amuse?
- To share?
- To convince?
- Other?

Therefore, my purpose for writing is:

_____

_____

_____

Next, consider your audience.

Am I writing for:

- Someone who knows very little about my topic? ___
- Someone who is an expert on my topic? ___
- Someone who is much younger than I? ___

Therefore, my audience is:

_____

_____

_____

May be reproduced for classroom use only.

	Note-sheet Graphic Organizer for Researching Feature Article Stories		
	Source 1 Title/Web site:	Source 2 Title/Web site:	Source 3 Title/Web site:
Idea/Question			
Idea/Question			
Idea/Question			

May be reproduced for classroom use only.

Graphic Organizer for the Feature Article
Rough Draft

Introduction or short anecdote providing background information:

_____

_____

_____

_____

Body: Choose graphic organizer to suit text structure.
(Sample below includes one for the pros and cons of an issue.)

Pros	*Cons*

Concluding main points:

_____

_____

_____

_____

May be reproduced for classroom use only.

Model Essay: Narrative Procedure

May be reproduced for classroom use only

HOW TO WRITE A NARRATIVE PROCEDURE
by Katherine Laura Canole

Writing a narrative procedure is easy if you know the correct steps. I bet you know much more about this type of writing than you think you do, but I'd like to give you a few hints to remind you of things you may have forgotten. To write a narrative procedure, you will need three things: paper, pen (or pencil), and a fairly extensive amount of knowledge of your topic.

The first step to writing such a piece of work is choosing your topic. Once you have a topic you must choose your audience and set your purpose. The next step can be fairly extensive; you must brainstorm about your selected topic. Be sure to record all of your ideas so that you can decide whether or not you know enough about the topic to explain it to someone else. Once you have your ideas on paper you must organize them using a graphic organizer. When your organization is complete the hard part is over.

Now it is time to begin your first draft. If you have clear and detailed notes, this should be fairly easy. An important part of drafting is developing a "lead" or an interesting first line. If you don't catch your reader's attention right away, he or she may choose to look through the bookshelves for something better to read. After your lead is developed you will write an introduction to launch your reader into the purpose of your paper.

After completing your introduction you are ready to begin listing your steps, or drafting your steps in paragraph form. Be sure to write your steps in the correct order so your reader does not get confused. Between each step you must include a transition word, or phrase, to bridge, or connect your steps together, making them easier to follow. After including all of the necessary steps, check to make sure that you have been clear and to the point. Check to see if you are missing any information that is necessary to the reader. For example, you must include definitions for unfamiliar terms, or examples to clarify your topic. You may even choose to add a glossary at the end of your essay if there are several unfamiliar terms. Sometimes it is helpful to include a picture, graphic, map, or reference to assist your reader in his or her understanding. Once you have completed your draft, read your essay aloud to make sure that it makes sense to you.

Now comes the fun part: peer revision. Trade papers with a partner and read them aloud. Discuss your papers using constructive criticism. Do not write on your partner's paper; that is his job, but be sure to give your opinions about his paper. You may recommend some things to help your partner improve his paper or you may ask questions for further clarification. Note the purpose, audience, and some specific words that help illustrate the purpose and audience of your partner's paper.

When you get your own paper back, revise any sections that remain confusing. You may cross out, add additional lines, or change whole paragraphs. Don't leave writing that is not your best.

Finally, look for any areas that need editing. Fix any spelling, grammar, or sentence structure errors; you may work with your partner for this as well. Once you are confident with your paper, you can write or type a final draft. If you follow these easy steps, soon the process of writing a narrative procedure will become second nature and you will no longer need your teacher's help.

Elements of a Narrative Procedure

1. *A good narrative procedure is well organized.* The paper includes a clear introduction, body, and conclusion. In addition, there are clear transitions between each section.

2. *A good narrative procedure has a clear purpose.* The paper begins by stating the task being explained so the reader immediately understands the purpose of your paper.

3. *A good narrative procedure has logical steps.* The steps of the procedure are clear and easy to follow. They are based on fact, expert opinions, and/or personal experiences.

4. *A good narrative procedure has a clearly defined audience.* The audience, or for whom the writer is writing, should be clear and consistent throughout the paper. Writers must choose if they are writing for someone who has no experience with the procedure, some experience, or much experience. Writers must choose just one audience, the novice or the expert, and be consistent throughout the paper.

5. *A good narrative procedure has correct use of English language conventions.* The writer demonstrates an understanding of all rules of the English language.

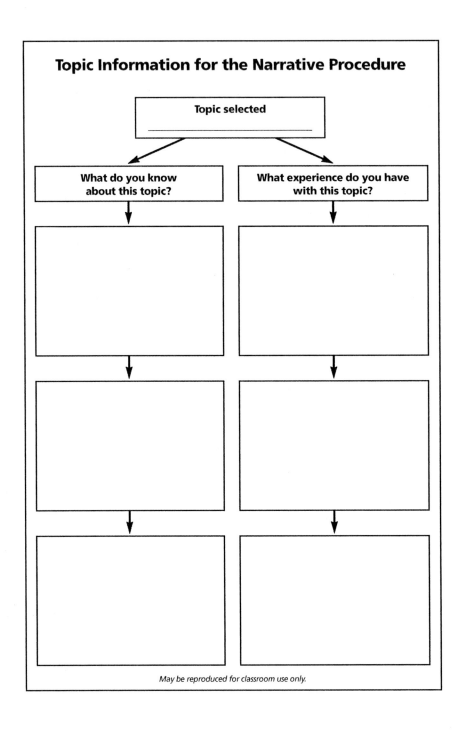

Topic Information for the Narrative Procedure

Topic selected

What do you know about this topic?

What experience do you have with this topic?

May be reproduced for classroom use only.

Determine Your Audience for the Narrative Procedure

1. **For whom** am I writing?

2. **What age are my readers?**
   Are they older, younger, or the same age as I am? The answers to these questions will help you decide the type of words to use. The vocabulary you choose will reflect the skill level of the reader.

3. **Are my readers beginners or experienced with this topic?**
   These answers will help you to determine how much, or how little detail you need in your writing. If a reader is a beginner, you will need to include much background knowledge. If your reader is experienced you will need less background knowledge, appealing to his or her expertise.

4. **What will be the most complex piece of the topic for my reader?**
   This answer will help you to establish the areas that you will need to provide more details and examples to assist your readers.

May be reproduced for classroom use only.

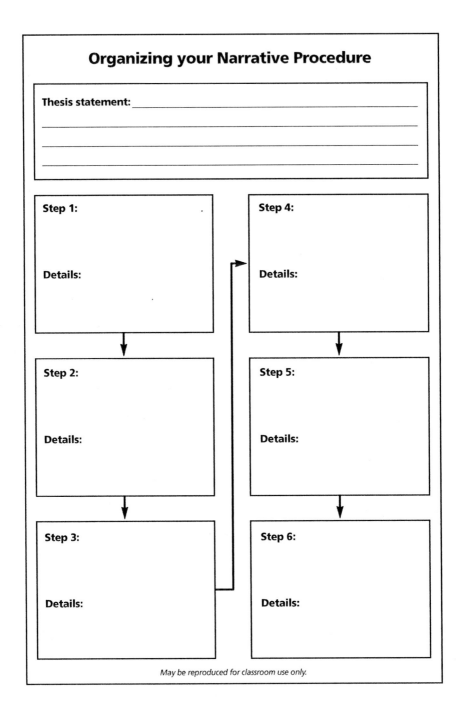

Organizing your Narrative Procedure

Thesis statement: _____

_____

_____

_____

Step 1:

Details:

Step 2:

Details:

Step 3:

Details:

Step 4:

Details:

Step 5:

Details:

Step 6:

Details:

May be reproduced for classroom use only.

Elements of a Math Response

- Writing should include responses to all parts of the question.
- There should be connections between each step.
- Each part of the question should be labeled.
- Organization should match the sequential nature of answering the question.
- The sequence of steps to solve and the strategy used should be included.
- The writing explains to the reader each step of the process needed to solve the problem.
- Mathematics content specific vocabulary is used throughout the response.
- The writing includes graphs, charts, number lines and diagrams as needed.
- Definitions for vocabulary words are included to demonstrate understanding.
- There needs to be evidence of computation with correct results.
- Editing is important! The writing demonstrates an understanding of spelling, grammar and mechanics.

May be reproduced for classroom use only.

Questions to Ask to Help Determine Your Math Response Audience

- Does the person reading this have the same degrees of mathematical knowledge as I do? Do they have more or less?
- Do they share a common math vocabulary with me? Do I need to explain the meanings of vocabulary?
- Did this person already solve this problem? Is my purpose to show evidence that I can solve the problem?
- Is my audience my teacher, peers, younger children, or adults?
- Is my reader assessing my knowledge? or Am I simply explaining the process to my readers?

May be reproduced for classroom use only.

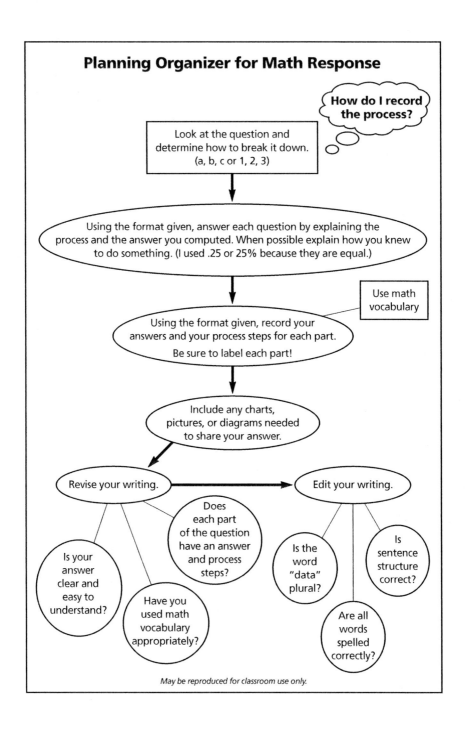

Planning Organizer for Math Response

How do I record the process?

Look at the question and determine how to break it down. (a, b, c or 1, 2, 3)

Using the format given, answer each question by explaining the process and the answer you computed. When possible explain how you knew to do something. (I used .25 or 25% because they are equal.)

Use math vocabulary

Using the format given, record your answers and your process steps for each part.

Be sure to label each part!

Include any charts, pictures, or diagrams needed to share your answer.

Revise your writing.

Edit your writing.

Does each part of the question have an answer and process steps?

Is your answer clear and easy to understand?

Have you used math vocabulary appropriately?

Is the word "data" plural?

Is sentence structure correct?

Are all words spelled correctly?

May be reproduced for classroom use only.

Annotated Final Draft Model Part I

Name _____

Date _____ Class _____

Reminder!
Answer and label each part.

Task:

- Answer all parts of the question.
- Answer in an organized and focused manner.
- Include appropriate details (for example, diagrams, charts, tables, definitions).
- Use math vocabulary to the best of your ability.
- Complete computations carefully and accurately.
- Explain the main ideas in your writing.
- Demonstrate your best mechanics and grammar.
- Include all stages of the process.

Question:

A group of students recorded the attendance data for their homeroom over two weeks. The results are shown in this table.

Homeroom Attendance Data

Date	Students Present (Total 21 students)
December 5	19
December 6	21
December 7	20
December 8	19
December 9	18
December 12	17
December 13	19
December 14	15
December 15	16
December 16	20

Use your math vocabulary!

A. Create a table using the above information that will show the attendance data as a fraction and as a percent.
B. Create a stem and leaf plot of the attendance data using the percentages.
C. What is the mode of the attendance data?
D. What is the mean of the attendance data?
E. What is the median of the attendance data? Show or explain your work.

Annotated Final Draft Model Part II

Response

A.

Date	Students Present (Total 21 students)	Fraction of students present	Percent of students present
December 5	19	19/21	90%
December 6	21	21/21	100%
December 7	20	20/21	95%
December 8	19	19/21	90%
December 9	18	18/21	86%
December 12	17	17/21	81%
December 13	19	19/21	90%
December 14	15	15/21	71%
December 15	16	16/21	76%
December 16	20	20/21	95%

➡ **Notice how the opening sentence restates the question.**

The table above shows the attendance **data** as **fractions** and as **percents**. *I found the **fraction** by recording the number of students present over the total number of students.* The number of students present is the **numerator** because it is the number of parts of the whole that are being considered. The total number of students is the **denominator** because it is the number of parts that make up the **whole**. *I found the percent of students present by **dividing** the **numerator** by the **denominator** and changing the **quotient** to a **decimal**.* My **quotients** were **decimals**. I know that .90 is read ninety hundredths, which is equal to 90%.

Example:

$19 \div 21 = .904761$ which when rounded to the nearest tenth is .90

$.90 = 90/100 = 90\%$

- **Math vocabulary is in bold**
- *Thinking processes are in italics*

B.

90	71
100	76
95	81
90	86
86	90
81	90
90	91
71	95
76	95
95	100

May be reproduced for classroom use only.

Annotated Final Draft Model Part III
Homeroom Attendance Percentages

Opening sentence restates question.

Stem	Leaf
7	16
8	16
9	00155
10	0

B. I created a stem and leaf **plot** of the attendance **percentages**. *To do this I first listed the* **data** *from* **least** *to* **greatest**. *Next, I used the numbers in the* **tens** *or* **hundreds** *place as my stem and the numbers in the ones place as my leaves.*

C. The **mode** of the students present is 90%. **Mode** is the **value** that appears most often in the **data**. 90% appears three times.

D. The **mean** of the attendance data is 87%. **Mean** is the **average** of a set of numbers. *To find the* **mean** *I found the* **sum** *of the attendance* **percentages** *and* **divided** *by the number of* **percents**.

```
   90
  100         874 ÷ 10 = 87.4
   95
   90         87.4 rounded to nearest whole number is 87
   86
   81
   90
   71
   76
 + 95
  ―――
  874
```

E. The **median** of the attendance **data** is 90%. The **median** is the middle **value** in a list of **statistics** ordered from **least** to **greatest**. *To find this I listed the* **data** *from* **least to greatest** *and found that 90 is the* **percentage** *in the middle.*

90	71
100	76
95	81
90	86
86	90
81	90
90	91
71	95
76	95
95	100

- **Math vocabulary is in bold**
- *Thinking processes are in italics*

May be reproduced for classroom use only.

Model Reflective Essay

May be reproduced for classroom use only

TERRORISM'S ANSWER
by Audrey G. Rocha

Natural disasters strike, lives are lost, and people ask, "What can I do to help?" When the disaster is of the manmade kind, the question seems that much more important. Although the word terrorism is relatively new, the concept is not. Terrorism has existed since man took up arms against each other. When on September 11, 2001 planes crashed into one of the Twin Towers in New York, everyone sadly looked on believing they were observing a terrible accident. Two minutes later another plane struck the other tower and people were incredulous, "Could it really have been two accidents? Is it coincidental?" People tuned into national and local television stations to see the footage being played over and over again. People who got out of the buildings were in shock. The nation was unsure of what was happening or of what to do. Then the Pentagon was hit. Finally, more reports came in about a plane headed for the White House that was somehow heroically brought down by passengers who banded together to fight back. Everyone aboard was lost, including the terrorists who overtook the plane. It was too devastating to comprehend.

Desperately I called my family. I was sure this was the end. Armageddon. My mom couldn't come home from work but assured me everything was okay and that I should stay in school. I was petrified. Watching the news all afternoon was both mesmerizing and dreadful. Replays of the day seemed like a movie being run over and over, but it wasn't. It was real life, a page of history, being played out right in front of us. These were real people, not actors in a mega-hit movie. I lost hope that any survivors would be found, including the fireman and police officers that were the first to respond to try to help people who were stuck in the buildings. Incredulous as it was, people were rescued from the rubble. Unreal stories of how people helped each other to get out of the buildings, how a stairway became a safe-haven, and stories of survival that were better than any I had ever read about.

My school organized a drop off spot for people in our town to bring goods desperately needed by the volunteers who left their jobs to help NYC dig out of the mess. The generosity of my town was stunning. Three truckloads were sent off filled with supplies. Celebrities later held a telethon to raise money for the families of the victims. The charity of the American people was awesome. Later, the President requested that at the designated time, everyone should leave their houses to light a candle in support of the thousands who were lost. As we stepped out of our houses to take part in this ritual, I noticed some of my neighbors. Some of them who never even spoke to each other were crying and hugging. It was then that I realized that in times of trouble people need to lean on each other. It is only in this act of support and strength that we can get through any disaster, natural or manmade.

Elements of a Reflective Essay

1. The piece is written in the first person voice.
2. The body of the paper hints at the author's opinion.
3. The author uses a subtle and reflective tone.
4. The piece should incorporate reflective language: "I think about"; "I wonder"; "I'm interested in knowing."
5. There is no "moral to the story."
6. The author's opinion is included in the concluding paragraph; it may be stated directly or simply hinted.
7. The reflective essay is based on the author's own experience; it is through this experience that the author derives meaning.

May be reproduced for classroom use only.

Brainstorming Topics for the Reflective Essay

People/Things	Places	Events

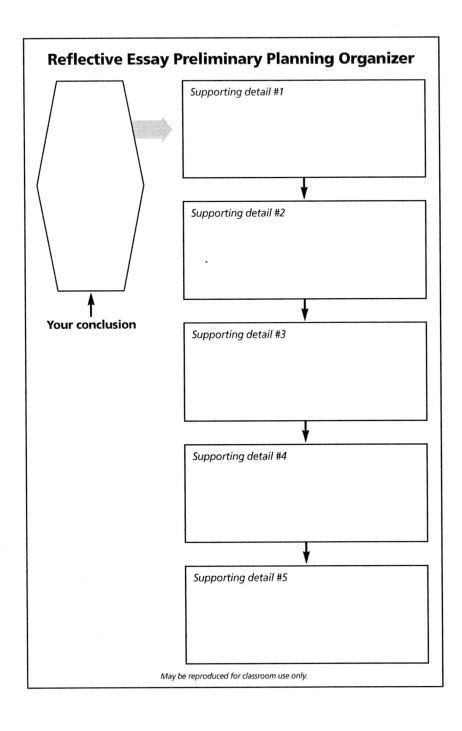

Reflective Essay Preliminary Planning Organizer

Supporting detail #1

Supporting detail #2

Your conclusion

Supporting detail #3

Supporting detail #4

Supporting detail #5

Choosing an Audience for Your Reflective Essay

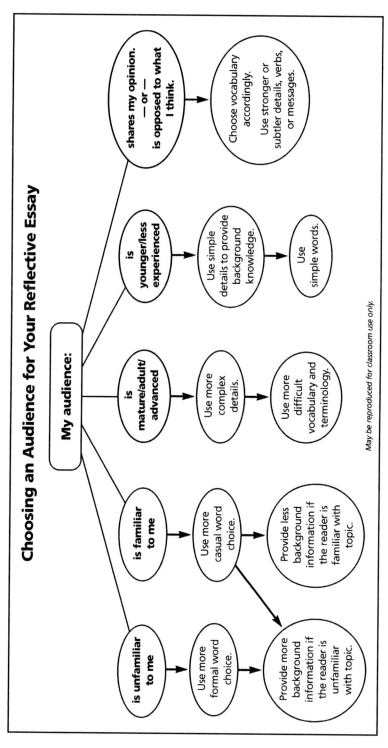

My audience:

is unfamiliar to me
→ Use more formal word choice.
→ Provide more background information if the reader is unfamiliar with topic.

is familiar to me
→ Use more casual word choice.
→ Provide less background information if the reader is familiar with topic.

is mature/adult/advanced
→ Use more complex details.
→ Use more difficult vocabulary and terminology.

is younger/less experienced
→ Use simple details to provide background knowledge.
→ Use simple words.

shares my opinion. — or — is opposed to what I think.
→ Choose vocabulary accordingly.
Use stronger or subtler details, verbs, or messages.

May be reproduced for classroom use only.

Model Expository Summary

May be reproduced for classroom use only

In 1793, doctors believed in the healing power of nature. They used gentle procedures, such as teas and brandy. They also used more drastic procedures such as phlebotomy, or bloodletting, which was an ancient medical practice. During this procedure, doctors would drain a small amount of the ill person's blood to hopefully make the remaining blood flow more freely. Bloodletting was used for a variety of illness including yellow fever (Murphy 59).

WORKS CITED

Murphy, J. (2003). *An American plague, the true and terrifying story of the yellow fever epidemic of 1793.* New York: Clarion Books, p. 59.

Elements of an Expository Text Summary

A good written summary...

- Contains a topic sentence that explains what the text is about. The topic sentence should be written in your own words.
- Contains all the main ideas of the text and only the very important details.
- Does not repeat any information.
- Does not include any trivial or unimportant information.
- Uses verbs suggesting a category instead of a list of verbs. For example, if your text is about sports, use the word, *"exercise,"* instead of listing all the types of exercise such as *"running, weightlifting, and jump-roping."*
- Uses nouns suggesting a category instead of a list of items. For example, if your text is about sports, use the word *"equipment,"* instead of *"weights, mats, and exercise balls."*

Adapted from (Brown & Day, 1983).

May be reproduced for classroom use only.

Modeling the Parts of a Summary

Paraphrased the topic sentence from the original text
↓

In 1793, doctors believed in the healing power of nature.
They used gentle procedures, such as teas and brandy. ◄——— **Main idea 1**
They also used more drastic procedures such as phlebotomy, ◄—— **Main idea 2**
or bloodletting, which was an ancient medical practice. ◄—— **Important detail**
During this procedure, doctors would drain a small amount ◄—— **Important**
of the ill person's blood to hopefully make the remaining **detail**
blood flow more freely. Bloodletting was used for a ◄——
variety of illnesses including yellow fever (Murphy 59). **Important detail**

↑
Reduced list of illnesses to a common noun, "variety"

Also, the length of the summary is significantly shorter than the text. The original text = 189 words; the summary = 70 words.

This summary is based on an excerpt from *AN AMERICAN PLAGUE, The True and Terrifying Story of the Yellow Fever Epidemic of 1793* by Jim Murphy. Copyright © 2003 by Jim Murphy. Reprinted by permission of Clarion Books, an imprint of Houghton Mifflin Company. All rights reserved.

May be reproduced for classroom use only.

Expository Text Structures
to Prepare for Summary Writing

Classification or Description

The main ideas are classified and described. For example, if the text were about whales, the information may be organized to describe sperm whales, killer whales, and right whales.

Sequence

The main ideas are organized sequentially. For example, the text may describe step by step how a baleen whale filters its food.

Comparison/Contrast

The information is organized to identify similarities and differences among main topics. For example, the text may describe the similarities and differences between whales and dolphins.

Cause and Effect

The main ideas are organized to identify causes and effects of a certain phenomena. For example, the text may describe the causes of whale disease, or it may describe the effects of an oil spill on a whale population or the causes and effects of the migration of a certain population for whales.

Problem/Solution

The main ideas are organized by problems and solutions. For example, the text may describe the problems of whale extinction and the solutions scientists are attempting to save a certain whale population.

May be reproduced for classroom use only.

Model Text for Expository Summary

May be reproduced for classroom use only

Several of the worst oil spills in recent times have been recorded in marine history. In 1997, there were three oil spills in Asia that affected shellfish and beaches. On January 7, in Japan, a Russian tanker leaked 5,200 tons of heavy fuel oil on beaches and threatened shellfish beds. On July 2, also in Japan, a tanker leaked 1500 tons of crude oil onto a fishing ground famous for its seafood. Lastly in 1997, on October 15, a huge tanker, which was carrying 120,000 tons of fuel leaked and coated several smaller islands off Singapore.

From 1998-1999, there were three more significant oil spills in Nigeria and Australia. On January 12,1998, the largest oil spill in Nigeria (40,000 barrels) threatened fish and destroyed fishing nets. In 1999, Australia was affected by two significant spills. The first spill, on June 28, occurred when a faulty pipe coupling caused 270,000 liters of crude oil to spill, damaging beaches and killing marine life. The second occurred on August 3, when a harbor was destroyed while an oil ship was unloading and a breach in the ship caused 80,000 liters of light crude oil to leak ("Snapshot oil spill").

WORKS CITED

Snapshop Oil Spill History, March 8, 2005. Whales Online. Available at: http://www.whales-online.org

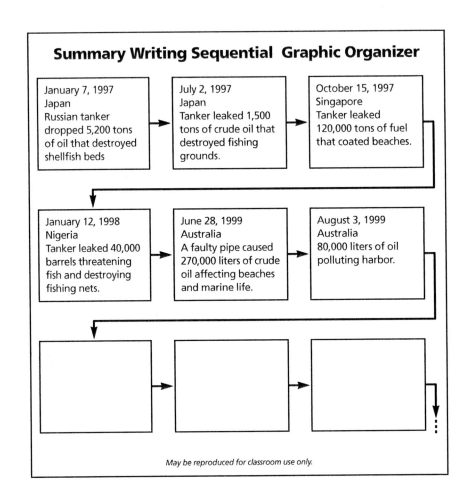

Summary Writing Sequential Graphic Organizer

| January 7, 1997 Japan Russian tanker dropped 5,200 tons of oil that destroyed shellfish beds | July 2, 1997 Japan Tanker leaked 1,500 tons of crude oil that destroyed fishing grounds. | October 15, 1997 Singapore Tanker leaked 120,000 tons of fuel that coated beaches. |

| January 12, 1998 Nigeria Tanker leaked 40,000 barrels threatening fish and destroying fishing nets. | June 28, 1999 Australia A faulty pipe caused 270,000 liters of crude oil affecting beaches and marine life. | August 3, 1999 Australia 80,000 liters of oil polluting harbor. |

May be reproduced for classroom use only.

Summary Writing:
Common Text Structure Signal Words

Classification or Description

many, several, one, another, still another
one type, another type
also, among, in addition to

Sequence

first, second, third, fourth
first, next, then, finally
in 2004, 2005, 2006 (any sequence of dates)
yesterday, today, tomorrow
steps, sequence, later, before, after, to begin
time, history

Comparison/Contrast

compare, comparison, contrast
same, different, like, as
similarities, differences, similarly
but, also
on one hand, on the other hand

Cause and Effect

cause(s), effect(s)
as a result of, result(s)
affect of, consequence of, consequently, therefore
for this reason

Problem/Solution

problem(s), issue(s)
solution(s), resolution(s), to resolve

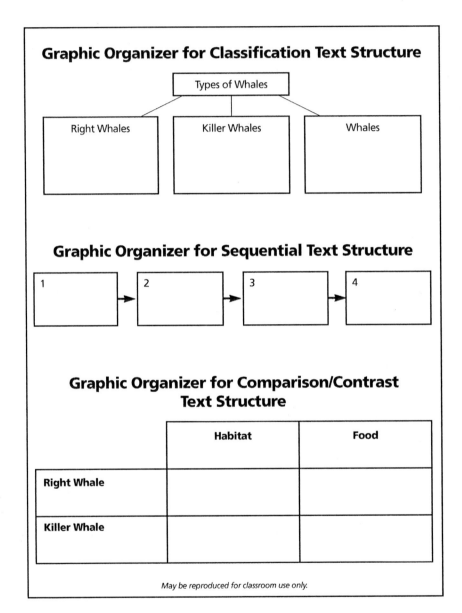

Graphic Organizer for Classification Text Structure

Types of Whales

Right Whales

Killer Whales

Whales

Graphic Organizer for Sequential Text Structure

1

2

3

4

Graphic Organizer for Comparison/Contrast Text Structure

	Habitat	Food
Right Whale		
Killer Whale		

May be reproduced for classroom use only.

Graphic Organizer for Cause/Effect Text Structure

Causes   **Effects**

Graphic Organizer for Problem/Solution Text Structure

Problems	⟶	Solutions
	⟶	
	⟶	

May be reproduced for classroom use only.

Summary Writing: Graphic Organizer for Classification Text Structure

Summary Writing: Graphic Organizer for Sequential Text Structure

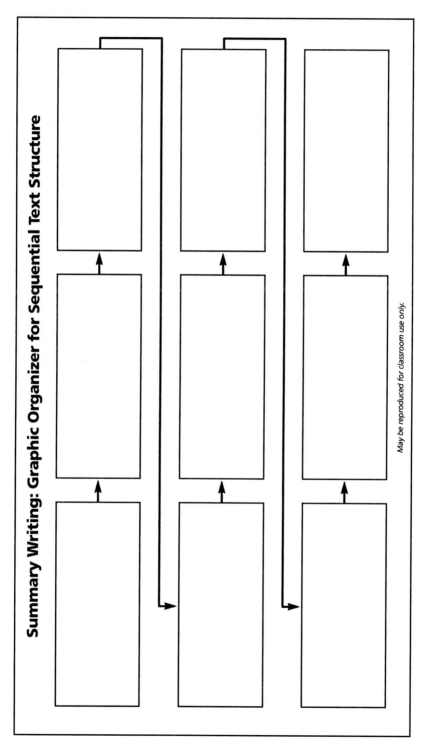

Summary Writing:
Graphic Organizer for Comparison/Contrast
Text Structure

Summary Writing:
Graphic Organizer for Cause/Effect Text Structure

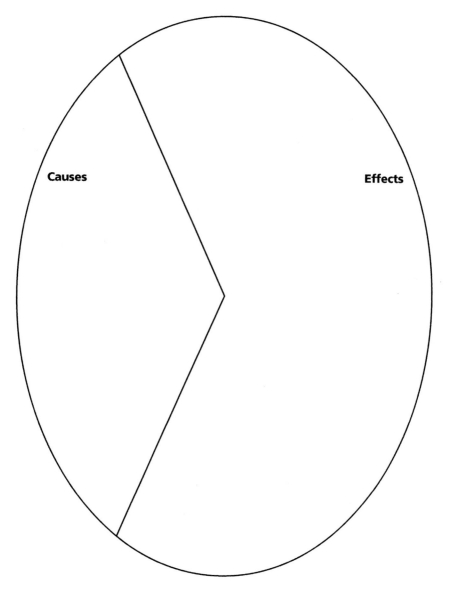

Causes   **Effects**

Summary Writing:
Graphic Organizer for Problem/Solution
Text Structure

Problem(s)	Solution(s)

Summary Writing:
Text Structure Practice Paragraphs

May be reproduced for classroom use only

CLASSIFICATION OR DESCRIPTION

Cetaceans (whales, dolphins, and porpoises) live in a marine environment that is threatened by many outside factors. *One* of the threats is change in climate. Within Polar Regions, melting ice causes ocean currents to change that can trigger a domino effect, such as temperature change, which will, in turn, change the marine ecosystem. *Another* threat to cetaceans is habitat loss caused by rising sea levels from climate and temperature change.

In addition to natural changes, pollutions will *also* affect the life of cetaceans. *One type,* chemical pollution caused by oil spills and industrial wastes, are toxins to whales, dolphins and porpoises. Another type of pollution that is affecting the marine life population is hard waste pollution. It has often been documented that coastal dolphins become tangled in fishing nets, plastic bags, fishing line, and off shore nets. This hard waste pollution can kill or disfigure these animals.

Lastly, *another* danger to marine life is the fishing industry. Fishing driftnets are still used around the world. These driftnets are made from rope that whale and dolphins do not easily detect. Many swim into these nets and are killed ("Living in Water").

SEQUENCE

Several of the worst oil spills in recent *times* have been recorded in marine *history.* In *1997,* there were three oil spills in Asia that affected shellfish and beaches. On *January 7,* in Japan, a Russian tanker leaked 5,200 tons of heavy fuel oil on beaches and threatened shellfish beds. On July 2, also in Japan, a tanker leaked 1500 tons of crude oil onto a fishing ground famous for its seafood. Lastly in *1997,* on *October 15,* a huge tanker, which was carrying 120,000 tons of fuel leaked and coated several smaller islands off Singapore. From *1998–1999*, there were three more significant oil spills in Nigeria and Australia. On *January 12, 1998*, the largest oil spill in Nigeria (40,000 barrels) threatened fish and destroyed fishing nets. *In 1999*, Australia suffered through two significant spills. The first spill of the year on June 28 occurred when a faulty pipe coupling caused 270,000 liters of crude oil to spill, damaging beaches and killing marine life. The second occurred on *August 3*, when a harbor was destroyed while an oil ship was unloading and a breach in the ship caused 80,000 liters of light crude oil to leak ("Snapshot oil spill").

CAUSE AND EFFECT

W hales, porpoises, and dolphins are highly *affected* by the *results* of chemical pollution. The main source of chemical pollution is from illegal waste dumping at sea, run-off chemicals used in agriculture, and oil spills.

Chemical pollution may *cause* disease, destroy food supplies, and natural habitats. Some chemicals are so toxic, they may even *cause* death. Chemical pollutants hurt marine animals by accumulating in the body tissue while they are feeding and are passed on through mother's milk. Most animals *affected* are those who are found along coastlines and feed on other animals in the food chain that may also have been *affected* by the chemical pollution ("Chemical and Nutrient Pollution").

COMPARISON/CONTRAST

M any types of pollution affect whales, dolphins, and porpoises. The *differences* between noise pollution and chemical pollution are vast, but *both* have *similar* effects on these marine animals.

Chemical pollution may cause disease, destroy food supplies and natural habitats. Some chemicals are so toxic, they may even cause death. Chemical pollutants hurt marine animals by accumulating in the body tissue while they are feeding and are passed on through mother's milk. Most affected are those who are found along coastlines and feed on other animals in the food chain that may also have been affected by the chemical pollution ("Chemical and Nutrient Pollution").

Noise pollution in the form of underwater blasts from military sonar or seismic testing can travel over 100 km. These loud noises are more damaging to whales, porpoises, and dolphins than previously thought. Research suggests that seismic blasts can kill marine animals that are too close. In addition, some blasts have been documented to cause lung and sinus hemorrhages causing disease or maybe even death of the marine animal. Perhaps the most documented detriment of noise pollution is the interruption of the marine animal's sonar capabilities. This interference threatens the marine animal's survival ("Noise Pollution"). Although noise and chemical pollution are very *different*, they are *similar* in nature because *both* cause harm by being potential hazards to the health and well being of cetaceans.

PROBLEM/SOLUTION

There are four solutions that environmentalists typically try when an oil spill occurs. One solution is called the "monitor-only" approach. This solution is, at the moment, considered "best practice" only when the water is deep and the location is considered remote. Another solution to contain oil spills is called the "mechanical containment" approach. In this approach, cleanup crews use booms and skimmers to contain the oil. This solution only works when the spill is small and seas are calm. A third solution is the "insitu burning oil" approach. This solution is considered dangerous because as the oil is set on fire, it creates substantial toxic air pollution. Lastly, for shoreline spills, environmentalists use the "shore-line clean-up" approach in which they mechanically remove oily sand from beaches and shorelines ("Internationally recognized").

WORKS CITED

Chemical and Nutrient Pollution, March 8, 2005. Whales Online. Available at: http://www.whales-online.org/

Internationally Recognized Spill Clean Up Solutions, March 8, 2005. Whales Online. Available at: http://www.whales-online.org/

Living in Waters of Trouble, March 8, 2005. Whales Online. Available at: http://www.whales-online.org/

Noise Pollution, March 8, 2005. Whales Online. Available at: http://www.whales-online.org/

Snapshop Oil Spill History, March 8, 2005. Whales Online. Available at: http://www.whales-online.org/

Strategy for Writing Expository Text Summaries

1. **Read** the text once through.
2. **Determine the topic** of the text.
3. **Identify the text structure** (the way the author arranged the ideas). If no text structure is evident, impose one.
4. **Draw an appropriate graphic organizer** to match the text structure you have chosen. For example:

Compare/Contrast

	Habitat	Food
Right Whale		
Killer Whale		

5. **Record the most important information** (main ideas) in the appropriate graphic organizer.
6. **Start drafting the summary** by writing a topic sentence that represents the main ideas of the text.
7. **Use the main ideas and important details** recorded in the graphic organizer to guide writing the remainder of your draft summary.
8. **Revise your draft** by:
   - locating and deleting trivial information.
   - locating and deleting information that is repeated.
   - checking to see if your topic sentence describes the overall meaning of the original text.
9. **Edit your draft** by proofreading for grammar, spelling, capitalization, and punctuation.
10. **Produce a polished final draft**.

May be reproduced for classroom use only.

REFERENCES

Bereiter, C., & Scadamalia, M. (1987). *The psychology of written composition.* Mahwah, NJ: Erlbaum.

Brown, A. L., & Day, J. D. (1983). Macrorules for summarizing texts: The development of expertise. *Journal of Verbal Learning and Verbal Behavior, 22,* 1–14.

Brown, A. L., Campione, J. C., & Day, J. D. (1981). Learning to learn: On training students to learn from text. *Educational Researcher, 10* (2), 14–21.

Calkins, L. M. (1994). *The art of teaching writing* (Rev. ed). Portsmouth, NH: Heinemann.

Environmental Protection Agency. (2003). *Trash in our oceans.* Retrieved February 1, 2005 from, http://www.epa.gov/owow/oceans/debris/index.html

Garner, R. (1987). *Metacognition and reading comprehension.* NJ: Ablex Publishing Corporation.

Georgia Department of Transportation (n.d.). *The dirty facts: Litter in Georgia.* Retrieved September 26, 2003, from http://www.stoplittering.com.

Gibaldi, J. (2003). *MLA Style manual and guide to scholarly publishing* (6th ed.). New York: Modern Language Association.

Graves, D. (1983). *Writing: teachers and children at work.* Portsmouth, NH: Heinemann.

Hairston, M., & Ruszkiewicz, J. J. (1991). *The Scott, Foresman handbook for writers.* New York: HarperCollins Publishers.

Hayes, J. R. (2000). A new framework for understanding cognition and affect in writing. In R. Indrisano & J. Squire (Eds.), *Perspectives on writing* (pp. 6–44). Newark, DE: International Reading Association.

Hayes, J. R., & Flower, L. S. (1980). Identifying the organization of writing processes. In L. Gregg & E. R. Steinberg (Eds.), *Cognitive processes in writing* (pp. 3–30). Hillsdale, NJ: Lawrence Erlbaum Associates.

Johnson, C. (1998). *Women of the Mayflower.* Retrieved February 2, 2005, from http://members.aol.com/calebj/women.html.

Johnson, C. (2000). *Girls on the Mayflower.* Retrieved February 2, 2005, from http://members.aol.com/calebj/girls.html.

Teaching Writing Genres Across the Curriculum, pages 201–202
Copyright © 2006 by Information Age Publishing
All rights of reproduction in any form reserved.

Johnson, C. (2003). *MayflowerHistory.com* Retrieved February 2, 2005, from http://www.mayflowerhistory.com/index.php.

Johnson, D. (2000). Just the right word: Vocabulary and writing. In R. Indrisano & J. Squire (Eds.), *Perspectives on writing* (pp. 162–186). Newark, DE: International Reading Association.

Kentucky Department of Education Division of Curriculum and Assessment Development (1997). *Open-response questions in the classroom.* Retrieved July 20, 2003, from http://www.kde.state.ky.us

Kintsch, W., & van Dijk, T. A. (1978). Toward a model of text comprehension production. *Psychological Review, 85,* 363–394.

Math Counts. (n.d.) *Problem solving strategies.* Retrieved July 29, 2003, from http://www.mathcounts.org/Problems/strategies.html

Meyer, B. J. F., & Rice, E. (1984). The structure of text. In P. D. Pearson (Ed.), Handbook of reading research (pp. 319–351). New York: Longman.

McCormack, R. L., & Pasquarelli, S. L. (1998). Literacy in the Elementary School II. *Unpublished course materials.* Bristol, RI: Roger Williams University.

Murphy, J. (2003). *An American plague, the true and terrifying story of the yellow fever epidemic of 1793.* New York: Clarion Books, p. 59.

National Center on Education and the Economy. (1997). *New standards performance standards* (Vol. 2). USA: Author, p. 24.

National Council of Teachers of Mathematics. (2000). Problem solving standard for grades 6–8. In *Principles and standards for school mathematics* (chap. 6). Retrieved July 29, 2003, from http://standards.nctm.org/document/chapter6/prob.htm

San Diego State University (n.d.). Elements of academic writing. *Common essay structures.* Retrieved July 23, 2003, from www.rohan.sdsu.edu/~capi/resources/Common.htm

Weaver, C. (1996). *Teaching grammar in context.* Portsmouth, NH: Heinemann.

Whales Online (2005). *Snapshop Oil Spill History.* Retrieved March 8, 2005, from http://www.whales-online.org.

White, D. (2002–3). Social studies for kids. *The American Revolutionary War: Keeping independence, Part 3: The end and the beginning.* Retrieved January 29, 2005, from http://www.socialstudiesforkids.com/articles/ushistory/revolutionarywar3.htm

ABOUT THE CONTRIBUTORS

Susan Lee Pasquarelli earned her doctoral degree in Language, Literacy and Cultural Studies from Boston University and is a Professor of literacy teacher education at Roger Williams University in Bristol, Rhode Island. Teacher education performance assessment has been the focus of her work for the last six years. In addition to designing performance assessment systems for RWU beginning teachers and graduate reading specialists, she has presented her work and associated research at regional and national conferences. Pasquarelli often provides in-service instruction to public school teachers that focus on the improvement of K–12 literacy instruction. Her public school work shaped the graduate writing instruction that informed all of the genre studies included in this book.

Linda B. Gambrell is Professor and Director of the School of Education at Clemson University. She began her career as an elementary classroom teacher and reading specialist in Prince George's County, Maryland. Her many publications include books on reading instruction and articles published in journals such as *Reading Research Quarterly, The Reading Teacher, Educational Psychologist,* and *Journal of Educational Research.* Gambrell has received professional awards including the 1998 International Reading Association Outstanding Teacher Educator in Reading Award, the 2001 National Reading Conference Albert J. Kingston Award, and the 2002 College Reading Associate Laureate Award. She is currently Vice-President Elect of the International Reading Association and will serve as President in 2007–08.

Michele Barlow was most recently a reading specialist at Pocasset Elementary School in Tiverton, Rhode Island before taking a leave of absence to start a family. Trained as a literacy coach, she worked with students and teachers to create reading and writing experiences aimed to improve class-

Teaching Writing Genres Across the Curriculum, pages 203–205
Copyright © 2006 by Information Age Publishing
203

room practice and, ultimately, student achievement. She earned a MA in Special Education from the College of New Rochelle and spent seven years teaching inclusive special education at the elementary level. She is currently taking literacy courses at Roger Williams University to earn her Rhode Island reading specialist/consultant certification.

Katharine L. Canole is an 8th grade English language arts teacher at Thompson Middle School in Newport, Rhode Island. She is currently working with a colleague to develop a clear, complete, and effective unit for teaching persuasive writing to middle school students. Once the unit is complete, she will begin filming each lesson and make them available for parents, colleagues, and students on the school website. Canole graduated from the Roger Williams University, MA in Literacy Program in May 2006 with honors.

Sue Dunbar is a 6th grade language arts and social studies teacher at Thompson Middle School in Newport, Rhode Island. She has also taught science at the middle level and strongly believes in integrating reading and writing throughout the content area. Currently she is a participant in Literacy Coach training through the East Bay Educational Collaborative, and with the assistance of the literacy coach at her school, her room was opened as a Lab classroom where other teachers are welcome to observe. Dunbar will graduate from the Roger Williams University, MA in Literacy Program, in May 2006.

Tara Fernandes is a Middle School Special Education Teacher at Southeast Alternative School in Berkley, Massachusetts. She works with a population of students diagnosed with social, emotional, and behavioral disorders. She is graduating from the Roger Williams University, MA in Literacy Program in May 2006.

Melissa Francis is an 8th grade language arts teacher at Kickemuit Middle School in Warren, Rhode Island. Currently, she is a member of her school's action team, ELA curriculum committee, and several other programs within the school. Team teaching with her school's literacy coach, Melissa will be the lead teacher in a lab classroom program partnered by a local educational collaborative. She will be graduating from Roger Williams University, MA in Literacy program in May 2006.

Megan Labrecque is a 6th grade special education teacher at Tiverton Middle School in Tiverton, Rhode Island. She supports her students in a resource and inclusion setting, in addition to teaching intensive reading, language arts, and mathematics. Currently, Ms. Labrecque is sharing her knowledge with the teachers in her building in order to improve current practices and to integrate literacy in all subject areas. Ms. Labrecque is graduating from the Roger Williams University, MA in Literacy Program, in May 2006.

Audrey Rocha graduated from the Roger Williams University, MA in Literacy Program in May 2006. She is currently a stay-at-home Mom but is planning to secure a position as an elementary classroom teacher and use her knowledge of literacy to enhance her own instruction. This semester, she is conducting a writing project with 9th grade English Language Arts students.

Suzanne Madden Scallin is a 6th grade math and science teacher at Roosevelt Middle School in New Bedford, Massachusetts. She has taught grades 3 through 8 in public and Catholic schools. She actively integrates literacy into her math and science classes and is currently on the School Improvement Team and the Literacy Curriculum committee. In May, 2005, Suzanne graduated from Roger Williams University, MA in Literacy Program with honors. Suzanne is the proud mother of three sons, Owen, Noah and Shane.

INDEX

Teaching Writing Genres Across the Curriculum, pages 207–210
Copyright © 2006 by Information Age Publishing